Alcoholism and Women

Marie-Louise von Franz, Honorary Patron

**Studies in Jungian Psychology
by Jungian Analysts**

Daryl Sharp, General Editor

Alcoholism and Women

The Background and the Psychology

JAN BAUER

Canadian Cataloguing in Publication Data

Bauer, Jan, 1943-
 Alcoholism and women

(Studies in Jungian psychology; 11)

Bibliography: p.
Includes index.

ISBN 0-919123-10-4

1. Women—Alcohol use.   2. Women—Alcohol use—
Treatment.   3. Women—Alcohol use—Case studies.
4. Women—Psychology.   5. Jung, C. G. (Carl
Gustav), 1875-1961.   I. Title.   II. Series.

HV5137.B38   362.2′92′088042   C82-095091-2

INNER CITY BOOKS
Box 1271, Station Q, Toronto, Canada M4T 2P4

Honorary Patron: Marie-Louise von Franz.
Publisher and General Editor: Daryl Sharp.
Editorial Board: Fraser Boa, Daryl Sharp, Marion Woodman.

INNER CITY BOOKS was founded in 1980 to promote the
understanding and practical application of the work of C.G. Jung.

Cover: Head of the young Dionysos, god of wine. Late Hellenistic
carving, found near Rome. (British Museum)

Glossary and Index by Daryl Sharp.

Printed and bound in Canada by Webcom Limited

CONTENTS

See last pages for descriptions of other INNER CITY BOOKS

Preface

When I was little and thought about what to do when I grew up, I decided I wanted to go to Africa and help Albert Schweizer. I also wanted to become a psychiatrist. In my mind these two plans were not necessarily related, for I really had no idea where Africa was or what Dr. Schweizer did, nor, for that matter, what it meant to be a psychiatrist. To me the important things were to understand, to *do* something in life, preferably helpful, and to get as far away as possible from where I was at that time. In context these fantasies were not surprising, for I grew up in an environment heavily affected by drinking and alcohol-related problems. As a child, however, I could neither understand, nor help, nor get away. It was only later that I could begin to do all three.

First a close family friend, himself a recovered alcoholic, began to talk with me about Alcoholics Anonymous and took me to open meetings where I could listen and learn about alcoholism from the people who knew best. That was the beginning of a new understanding of the confusion and contradictions I had grown up with.

Then I actually did get away. First to study and work in France and eventually to Switzerland, the birthplace at least of my childhood hero Dr. Schweizer. By then, however, my allegiance had changed. Not wanting to go to Africa or to attend medical school—which would have been necessary to become a psychiatrist—I still wanted to be in the so-called helping professions and understand more about the human psyche. So C.G. Jung replaced Dr. Schweizer and I trained to become an analyst.

During the years of training I was often struck by the similarities and parallels between the individual approach of Jungian analysis and the collective approach of Alcoholics Anonymous. Eventually it became a goal to somehow bring the two together in one work, showing how they could mutually support and complement each other in attempts to come to grips with the problem of alcoholism. This book is a product of that effort.

As for the particular focus on alcoholism in women, that comes from a combination of feminist tendencies and observations over the years about alcoholics of both sexes. Within and outside of AA meetings, I had noticed how often women's drinking stories were different from those of men and how much these differences were neglected or denied, not least by the women themselves who wanted to be accepted in the group. Something that impressed me, for example, was the repetition of the theme of secrecy in women's drinking. Unlike men, who more often worked their way into alco-

holism through business meetings and social contacts afforded by
bars and other public drinking spots, women almost invariably told
of behind-doors nipping, bottles hidden in laundry hampers and
kitchen cupboards.

Furthermore, once they had come out of the closet about their
drinking problem and achieved sobriety, they still related stories that
were quite different in many respects from the stories of the men
who had done the same. For instance, for every helpful and supportive wife who had stayed by her drunken husband and tried through
patience and understanding to help him in the initial and most
difficult period of sobriety, there was a husband who had either left
his drinking spouse before she became sober, or remained indiffer-
ent, if not outright hostile, to his wife's efforts at sobriety.

But in the literature on alcoholism these discrepancies were seldom mentioned. Alcoholism was treated as a uniform illness and the
implication was that it struck only men. If women were mentioned
at all, they were either included within the men's realm with no
special differentiation, or they were considered simply as much
sicker—aberrations or freaks. As these observations were confirmed
regularly by listening to women speak of their experiences, I decided
to write about the problem of alcoholism from the point of view of
the woman drinker.

Naturally, with such a subject one cannot speak only of one sex.
There are important general traits in both background and symptoms that are shared by all alcoholics and these are discussed also.
The same goes for attitudes of the public that affect alcoholics of
both sexes. The emphasis here, however, remains on the woman
drinker and the case stories concern only women alcoholics.

For the information of the reader, the appendix contains a list of
the Twelve Steps and Twelve Traditions as they appear in Alcoholics
Anonymous literature. The reader will also find there an exchange
of letters between Bill Wilson, cofounder of AA, and C.G. Jung.

Introduction

In 1978 there were approximately ten million alcoholics or problem drinkers in the United States, one-third of whom were women.[1] Among the one million members of Alcoholics Anonymous, the proportion was about the same, although the figures for women drinkers was rising and continues to rise among new members. Whatever the exact figures today, the number of women alcoholics is clearly increasing both in America and Western Europe, and alcoholism can no longer be considered uniquely a man's problem—literature and public opinion notwithstanding. Certainly the main reasons have to do with the deep social changes in traditional feminine and masculine roles. Until recently, although they were considered unequal and different, women at least had a subculture in which to evolve. In this maternal, female world, where feminine values prevailed, there was little opportunity for a sense of individual selfhood and autonomy, but at least it did provide a sense of collective gender solidarity and identity. Women could remain in that paradise in a more or less unconscious state, and men were happy to stay outside in the "real" world.

But now that subculture of women no longer exists—at least not in its original, inviolate state—and no amount of natural childbirth or breastfeeding, however laudable in themselves, can reverse the clock, any more than folklore demonstrations and fashionable minority studies can restore the cultures of the Indian or black tribes which were destroyed and then "rediscovered" by the white man. To continue the analogy, the breakdown of feminine culture has evolved in much the same way as that of those "less developed, less civilized" peoples—who also succumbed to alcohol, the white man's firewater, in epidemic numbers when their own values and history were annihilated.

Regrettable or not, the social upheavals of the last two hundred years have caused the modern world to encroach upon the conservative feminine sphere. The strongest, or luckiest, women have begun to break out of their insulating paradise, to seek a more conscious way and to engage in the traditionally male world of real power and influence. But their advances have brought them a share of not only the privileges of this world but the pathologies as well, alcoholism being one of the most widespread.

Those women who choose to stay behind, either out of real conviction or simply fear, are not, however, exempt from increasing invasion of their protective cocoon. Even if they muster all their polemic "animus" strength, like Anita Bryant and other back-to-the-

9

house advocates, in order to maintain the anatomy-determined destiny decreed for them, they are fooling themselves in believing that they defend a woman's world. For this is more and more a man's idea of a woman's world. In the name of technological progress and logos expertise, specialists are there at every turn to tell a woman how to be one. How to be a good wife, how to be a good mother—the instructions handed down by doctors and other authorities, who are supported, if not co-opted, by the enormous power of the advertising industry, are explicit and irrevocable. Even the traditional outsider woman, the Mistress, is now assimilated by the Establishment and told how to be what she is. Love-making and seduction are as codified in popular magazines as cooking and child-rearing. In spite of the real progress in women's rights and consciousness, there has never been such a time when so few are actually defined by their own values, either feminine or individual. If this seems inevitable for the working woman who chooses to enter a male-oriented world, it is no less true for those who remain behind.

The final irony comes not from the patriarchal figures in power but from those men who, at the urge of feminists and in the name of more role flexibility, are also anti-Establishment, who enter the woman's world and take up domestic tasks. That this choice is possible for men certainly expresses a positive breaking-down of rigid stereotypes. But the value put on this change for men, as opposed to the value put on the change for women, is revealing. Men, as loving, caring fathers and conscientious house-husbands fill the papers with their enthusiastic discoveries of the joys of domesticity. They are admired for having the courage to don their feelings and femininity. Women, on the other hand, are urged at all costs to be nonthreatening to men. They may be rewarded monetarily for having "masculine" characteristics, but more often than not they will pay for material equality with social and personal loss.

Thus the circle is completed and women are stuck in their own evolutionary process. They can't go backward into an illusory paradise of feminine innocence. Consciousness has been too dearly paid for, and besides, most of what is left of so-called feminine culture has been largely appropriated by masculine interest or mimicry. But nor can women just leap forward into total and literal "sameness." Neither men nor women are ready for this, nor is it necessarily the solution. For the moment, most women are simply stuck in a "no-woman's-land," where each tries to come to individual solutions, some more satisfactory than others. Usually these solutions entail sideways movements, attempts to find compromises or new, unorthodox ways of being female and human. Some of these lead to constructive, new ways of living. Others don't.

In any culture, when its members lose their inner sense of cohesion and orientation, they are also more subject to such outside ills as stress and addiction. Women are no exception. Ousted from their subordinate but safe position, they now qualify for what Jung claimed was particularly a man's illness. They are no longer "soft on the outside but hard on the inside," as Jung described them, with their male animus soul rooted firmly in traditional collective forms of the feminine role. Today they are as likely to be hard outside and unsure inside, and often unsure both inside and outside. Their animus is split, pulling them forward into an emancipated world, while dragging them simultaneously back into traditionally approved passivity.

When they seek to escape from this inner and outer push-pull of the masculine and to find a feminine guide, there are none, or very few. Just as the breakdown of the Christian culture and the failure of the institutionalized Church to keep up with contemporary spiritual needs accounts for much of the individual disorientation that leads to neurosis and social problems such as alcoholism, so the failure of more differentiated feminine role models to keep up with women's needs and provide them with guidelines, leaves them open to getting lost and overcome by other forces as they search for their new identities.

Clinical Aspects

Who are the women who choose alcohol as a "solution" to their problems, only to find themselves chosen by alcoholism? What do they do when they drink and what does drink do to them?

As with men, but even more, the picture is distorted by stereotypes that have arisen due to the shadow role that the alcoholic plays in society. Yet, contrary to these stereotypes, alcoholism in women is not limited to hysterical actresses, unkempt landladies and frustrated spinsters. The woman drinker may be a model housewife, an active professional or the wife of an American president.[2] In a brochure called "Alcoholics Anonymous for the Woman," for example, there are six "typical" portraits of women drinkers, yet none is typical in the sense of social stereotypes. They include a housewife, a writer, a prisoner, a singer, a doctor, and a hospital inmate. From the outside these women do not seem to have much in common. Their backgrounds differ as much as do their life styles. What they share is the compulsion they had to drink. As for what led to their addiction and how they lived it out, the patterns also vary.

Yet one can detect in the drinking careers of these women, and of any other alcoholic, certain classic character traits and drinking patterns that point to addictive rather than normal drinking. Various authors have studied and described such patterns. Neil Kessel and Henry Walton, a team of British psychiatrists, delineate more scrupulously than most the clinical progression from excessive to addictive to chronic alcoholic drinking. They even go so far as to break this progression down into 54 detailed steps, which can be summarized as follows:

1. *Excessive drinking* is marked by a preoccupation with drinking, a need for alcohol in order to function at work or in society, guilt and alibis and dishonesty about the consumption of alcohol.
2. *Addiction* is revealed, say the authors, by an increasing frequency of blackouts, financial deception and extravagance, absenteeism, social isolation and "the wife taking over more responsibilities."
3. Further on, such symptoms as morbid jealousy, reduction of sexual desire, morning drinking, suicide attempts and breakup of the family point to irreversible addiction. Then the last stage, *chronicity,* is marked by confused thinking, DT's, constant drinking and finally, with luck, "going to AA or seeking medical treatment."[3]

The references to the wife and sexual symptoms are clearly meant to evoke the picture of the classic male alcoholic. Even for a man, however, it is deceptive, for it implies that each one of the 54 stages must be lived through before the hapless individual finally turns for help, having hit the end of the road and lost his family, job, health and dignity. But experience in AA and modern approaches to alcoholism prove that it is not necessary for either man or woman alcoholic to hit such a drastic bottom before being ready to ask for help. Furthermore, although many of the stages of addiction as described are lived also by women, many are not. If the guilt, lack of self-esteem, remorse, irresponsibility and ultimate degradation are similar, the predominance of secret drinking among women and the relatively rare cases of really chronic alcoholism create a different picture from the classic male one.

On the other hand, from a clinical point of view the reasons that push women into drinking, and certain character traits likely to be found in women alcoholics, could be said to be similar to those of men alcoholics, regardless of individual background. Some of these factors are explored and cited in *Thirst for Freedom* by David A. Stewart. Using less jargon than Kessel and Walton, he reduces to five the reasons behind the urge to drink too much:

1. A desire to dull the pain of duty or personal relations.
2. To ease tension and anxiety.

3. To ease boredom and fatigue.
4. To release pent-up feelings.
5. To experience a release from the stiff prison of "adulthood" into the liberation of childlikeness, or, more often, childishness.

Further on, he mentions six core attributes that he finds prevalent in the personality structure of alcoholics of both sexes. Alcoholics, he says, are:

1. *Hypersensitive*—they are more susceptible than other individuals to both physical and psychological stimuli.
2. *Dependent*—from a deep-rooted lack of affective security, they have remained in certain ways emotionally immature, thence the need to cushion themselves from life and the regressive symptoms when intoxicated.
3. *Idealistic*—they alternate between inflation and deflation, overestimation of their capacities and debilitating self-denigration.
4. *Impulsive*—they are quick to seek instant gratification, not having had the primary security that allows for building up a level of frustration tolerance.
5. *Perfectionist*—they are critical of themselves and often defiant vis-à-vis authority figures.
6. *Wishful thinkers*—because of their own tyrannical perfectionism, they have to escape into fantasy in order to realize their dreams.[4]

Now, many people have such traits. In current psychological language, they could be called narcissistic. In Jungian language, they would generally be recognized as puer or puella types. But even within the narcissistic structure or the puer/puella pattern, there are different individual manifestations and variations, and not all become alcoholic. What differentiates alcoholics is simply that they drink to get drunk; they drink whether they want to or not; they have no control over their drinking; and once they begin, they are at more risk of letting go and expressing sides of themselves that others manage to keep under control or to express differently.

What happens to alcoholics in archetypal terms, as we shall see, is that under the influence of alcohol they become possessed by Dionysos, the god of intoxication. Given basic childhood insecurities plus a temperament that adapts with difficulty to collective norms, they experience a kind of tension of opposites between the accepted Apollonian ideals of society and the pull toward Dionysian revolt and disruption of these very same ideals. If the environment is "favorable," this tension will be resolved in alcohol and eventually alcoholism. However, this resolution is not just an abdication, or revolt *against*. Nor is it just the opposite, that is, an attempt, however illusory, to rise above personal insecurities and be "more" than the average member of conventional society. There is yet something else. As Stewart puts it:

> Deeper than concern for money, or interest in power, prestige or sex, deeper, too, than evidence of problems and pain, psychological or physical—is the search for something more in a positive experience, beyond alleviation of their troubles. [Alcoholics] simply express the ideals of every sensitive and imaginative human being in his depths.[5]

To find out what these ideals are is one aim of this book. To find out why, in the life of the alcoholic and especially the woman alcoholic, such ideals lead to alcoholism instead of some more creative activity—as ideals can and often do—is another aim.

Finding out means looking into, studying the context around a subject and the traits that characterize it. The medieval doctor and alchemist Paracelsus believed that in such an undertaking it is better to deal with perceived phenomena than with mere speculation, "for nature is what can be seen, but speculation . . . is what cannot be seen. . . . The seeable renders the truth. The unseeable renders nothing."[6]

However, Paracelsus as both a medical doctor dealing with matter and an inquirer into the alchemical mysteries, knew that seeing and perceiving include two vantage points: the objective and the subjective, the outer and the inner. In the foregoing cultural background and clinical description of alcoholic patterns, the outside view predominates. It will continue to be present in the following chapters—in a discussion of the development of different social attitudes to alcoholism and women alcoholics, in descriptions of different women's drinking stories and in case studies. But this book originated in personal reactions and observations, especially the conviction that not enough *subjective* material from and about alcoholic women is available to balance the masses of clinical descriptions and sociological graphs. What *has* been written in a more subjective vein has been largely literary (autobiographies or novels), often very enlightening but rarely consulted or taken seriously by the very people who make it their business to deal with the problem.

My principal aim, therefore, has been to write a book that contained something of both realities, the outer and the inner—to balance research concerned with outside facts and opinions with research into lived experiences and "inside" opinion, including my own and that of those who have been there, the women alcoholics who are the real authors of this book.

1

Medical Background and Theoretical Models

Alcoholism as Pathology

Alcoholism as a specific ailment only came into its own in the 19th century. It was the time of the Industrial Revolution and alcoholism was spreading in epidemic proportions, especially among the working classes. It was also, however, the century of scientific classification, when, under the influence of the goddess of reason, science and medicine began to order and diagnose illnesses, particularly mental illnesses, that had hitherto been the domain of the Church and society at large. Alcoholism was no exception to this fascination with order. Doctors everywhere exerted their efforts to describe and classify the condition, but few were interested in why people drank, and fewer still in the possible differences between men and women drinkers. In general, despite the veneer of objectivity that a certain logical classification lent to the subject, the attitude of those doctors who did concern themselves with alcoholism was dominated mainly by a moral point of view: alcoholism was considered more as a vice and symptom of moral degeneration than an illness.

There were a few exceptions. In America, a doctor by the name of George Beard spent years studying alcoholics. He came to the conclusion that the problem stemmed from an imbalance between energy expended and energy available. For him, alcohol was an artificial stimulant that permitted the individual—especially manual workers who formed the bulk of his research population—to work beyond his normal means.[7] Anyone who has ever been inspired to unusual physical or psychological efforts while "under the influence" will recognize this proposition. But at the time it was unusual in that Dr. Beard laid the emphasis on physical, not moral, causes.

In France, Pierre Janet, one of the pioneers in research into the unconscious, came to a somewhat similar conclusion, although he based his theory on psychological rather than physical tension, proposing that alcoholics were "psychasthenic" individuals who needed the excitement of some kind of addiction, even crime, to stimulate them into active life.[8] Later, after World War I, he made extensive studies on alcoholism from a social and national point of view, reflecting within his own system of ideas the shift in emphasis that took place from the 19th to the 20th century. This socio-cultural point of view was to prevail, along with more sophisticated psychological theories, up until the present day.[9]

15

Back in the 19th century, however, only a few others attempted to reconcile science and morality in their theories on alcoholism. In Vienna, another pioneer in the psychology of the unconscious, Alfred Adler, thought that alcoholism, like other psychological disorders, was the result of organ inferiority and a manifestation of his famous "masculine protest": through drinking the alcoholic escaped from the duties and responsibilities of community membership.[10]

In Switzerland, Auguste Forel, professor of psychiatry at Zürich University and reformer of the Burghölzli Mental Asylum, questioned why psychiatry, with its new discoveries about mental processes, still had no results with alcoholism. Since he received no satisfactory answers from his colleagues, he addressed himself to a cobbler who was known to have cured others and had himself been cured of alcoholism. The answer he gave Forel was: "No wonder, Herr Professor, I am an abstainer while you are not."[11]

From then on Forel did abstain from alcohol and was able to help many of the alcoholic patients he came upon in his practice. His method, which was more one of example than treatment, showed already that the psychological disposition of the healer was as important as actual techniques or theories. Such an attitude foresaw in many ways the success of the program of Alcoholics Anonymous which would only be founded some 50 years later. It also illustrates Jung's belief that the analyst must be involved, not as a superior being, but as a participant in a dialectical relationship where "in the foreground is the personality of the doctor himself as a curative or harmful factor," and therefore "what is now demanded is his own transformation."[12]

Aside from the work of these and a handful of other practitioners, however, alcoholism did not receive much attention from the avant garde of the 19th-century medical establishment. While students of the young science, psychiatry, made pilgrimages to see the famous Dr. Charcot and his performing hysterics at Salpetrière in Paris, no one lined up to see alcoholics in or out of institutions. Ordinary medical doctors faced with a person suffering from alcoholism continued as their forerunners had. They advised cures, perhaps better quality wines to their wealthier patients, and simply condemned the poorer ones to charitable institutions or undignified death—either alternative being the result of the "moral degeneracy" point of view that the conventional medical establishment shared with their social and cultural milieu.

It was only in the 20th century, beginning with the study by Janet in 1915, that other points of view began to develop and that social, psychological and cultural questions were approached, placing alcoholism in a broader, less moralistic context. Still, more than most illnesses, mental or physical, the very term alcoholism continued and continues still, to provoke moral reactions and controversy. It has been officially recognized as an illness by the World Health Organization since 1951. Yet, despite this recognition of alcoholism as an ailment and not a crime, there is still little consensus on exactly what it consists of. As Siegler and Osmand, authors of "Models of Alcoholism," put it:

> Alcoholism, like schizophrenia and drug addiction, is a disputed ailment. That is to say, it is an undesirable condition which is said by some to be a disease, by others a moral failing and by still others a psychological disturbance. It may also be identified as a social problem, an impairment, a faulty mode of family interaction or an inexplicable result of that pleasant activity, social drinking.[13]

There are as many points of view as there are kinds of people looking at the problem. The physician and the minister, the psychotherapist and the policeman, the social drinker and the alcoholic, all speak different languages and can offer explanations that make sense from their vantage point.

In an attempt to sort out this Tower of Babel, Siegler and Osmand applied the idea of models to alcoholism. The models are not in themselves comprehensive theories. They are simply frameworks in which theories develop and from which particular attitudes evolve. In good 19th-century tradition, in fact, they provide a kind of classification of theory, a concise and basic presentation of the different ways in which alcoholism can be and is approached.

My purpose in reviewing this schema is to both acknowledge and comment on existing attitudes toward the subject, including what is said or not about female alcoholism. In turn, the models will serve as references and a point of departure for the development of my own ideas. The models are abstractions, products of a thinking-type function that describes what a thing is. The authors do not attempt value judgments, nor do they give detailed examples of any theory. They simply provide an ordering system, a way to clarify the multiplicity of approaches and attitudes. I have filled in the various systems with examples and added my own subjective comments on these models, particularly how they relate to and influence women drinkers.

There are nine broad categories or models, reflecting different attitudes toward alcoholism:

The Impaired Model
The Dry Moral Model
The Wet Moral Model
The Alcoholics Anonymous Model

The Old Medical Model
The New Medical Model
Old Psychological-Analytic Models
New Psychological Models
The Family Interaction Model

The first four are lay models, that is, they are based on explanations of alcoholism by nonexperts. The last five are professional models, derived from schools and individuals who are considered authorities in the treatment and understanding of the problem.

Lay Models of Alcoholism

I shall pass briefly over the first three lay models in order to just give some idea of the common attitudes that come to bear upon the alcoholic in our society. As will be seen, these are as interesting for their omission of specific references to women drinkers as they are for what they do say about alcoholics in general.

The fourth lay model presents the AA concept of alcoholism as it began and evolved since its founding in 1935. This one I shall elaborate on more, since it forms the basis of my own observations and serves as a "laboratory" for the material presented in the latter part of the book.

The Impaired Model

From this point of view, the alcoholic is simply a drunk, sometimes repulsive, sometimes comical, but in any case irresponsible. Nice people do not really want to associate with such an individual. The cause of his condition is unknown. He just "is that way."

Since the prognosis is negative—that is, once a drunk always a drunk—treatment consists of charitable care given by kind individuals or such institutions as the Salvation Army or, eventually, state hospitals. The main thing is that the drunk is kept out of sight and out of trouble, whether this be undertaken by society or family.

Comment

This model presents the classic picture of the alcoholic as a social pariah, a Bowery bum or a derelict under a bridge. It reflects the die-hard Christian attitude toward alcoholism as a sin and the alcoholic as a fallen member of society. He should be pitied by the pious and more virtuous people. In fact, without the presence of such black sheep in society, do-gooders and upstanding citizens would have nothing to measure their own virtue by, so he plays a scapegoat role in carrying the collective shadow. The poet William Blake aptly summed up the necessity of such individuals with the lines:

> "And Pity no more could be
> If all were as happy as we."

This model of alcoholism as an impairment is the most traditional one in Western culture and to many people it would seem very old-fashioned. Yet, despite the fact that attitudes toward alcoholism have much evolved in recent years, it is surprising how widespread is the equation, alcoholic = derelict, with all the connotations of sin, irresponsibility and immorality such an image evokes. That this is true among the less educated strata of society might not be surprising, but in fact the reactions of supposedly more sophisticated individuals confronted with alcoholism in their own personal groups—or in themselves—show how much more prevalent the traditional view of impairment is than any more modern approach:

> "My husband can't be an alcoholic. He's never missed a day of work or laid a hand on me...."
>
> "I can't be alcoholic. I only drink after five o'clock in the evening and then only the best wines...."
>
> "I'm not alcoholic, I went to the best schools and belong to the most élite intellectual milieu...."

These are some of the spontaneous statements spoken by individuals when the problem threatens too close to home. Anything but an alcoholic. Immediately the age-old picture of the drunken bum, dressed in rags, smelly and incoherent, springs to mind, bringing with it the whole underside of our hygienic, responsible, work-ethic society.

For a woman, identification with this collective shadow has even worse consequences than for a man. First of all, this is due to the higher standards required of women in their social behavior, for in spite of the feminist movement, the role of women as the transmitters of social manners and virtues has not changed very much. They may work in a man's world, but they must not lose their femininity and must not lose their ability to fulfill their role as "civilizers."

Secondly, a woman is judged all the more severely within this framework because in some ways she is already considered impaired —just because she is female and the feminine is valued less than the masculine in most cultures. As long as she remained within her allotted role, this innate impairment at least made her eligible for lifelong support by a man. But as a drunk, not only has she fallen farther than the man but she has also flaunted the benevolence of masculine protection.

The Dry Moral Model

In this framework, alcoholism is a moral problem that only occurs because drinking occurs. The alcoholic behaves immorally because he drinks but if there were no alcohol available, the problem would be eliminated. Alcohol itself is the cause but the individual, unlike the drunk in the preceding model, is at least responsible for deciding to drink or not. As very few people can tolerate the effects of alcohol simply because of its intrinsic, mind-changing qualities, it is better to make alcohol unavailable and to make of any drinking a sinful activity.

In the extreme, this is a collective view that aims at changing society—in order to avoid the need to reform individuals. It might best be summed up by the law of Islam which describes fermented beverages as having "some good and some bad," but the bad is the greater part, therefore alcohol should be totally avoided.

The treatment of alcoholism under this model consists mostly of social and legal measures brought to bear on the individual to make one feel guilty for going against the "right" collective way.

Comment

As a model this is probably the least relevant in terms of influence on attitudes to alcoholism today. There are, of course, nations such as India and the Islamic countries where such a position is a normal collective one. But in our society the teetotallers are rare and temperance groups in the minority. Where they do exist, once again the standard for alcoholic women tends to be even stricter than that for men, so the women who are guilty of drinking must hide their problem behind a veil of secrecy and guilt.

The one time the dry moral model prevailed in our culture was during the Roaring Twenties, when Prohibition was in full swing. In a postwar loosening of sexual and social codes, many women began to drink liquor who would not have in the preceding generation. They drank it along with the men simply for the pleasure of indulging in forbidden fruit at the numerous speakeasies that sprouted up as soon as the law went into effect. But for them drinking was also proof of their belonging to a man's world and their right to partake in daring ventures beyond the traditional domestic cocoons they had been confined in by the Victorian standards of the 19th century.

Unfortunately, the tensions between the two conflicting social norms—the traditional, puritan Victorian and the new postwar Dionysian outbreak of the Twenties—was too great for many people. It culminated not only in the nationwide crash of 1929 but in an epidemic of individual collapses into alcoholism. A writer such as F.

Scott Fitzgerald, going from the peak of alcoholic glamour and glory to the depths of alcoholic despair is just one of the more well-known examples of what a whole society experienced. And even in the case of Fitzgerald, it is interesting to note that while he is looked upon as a tragic example of a talent succumbing to the dark side of Dionysos, his wife and drinking companion, Zelda, was simply considered crazy and benefited from little of the romantic aura that the public created around the alcoholism of her husband.

In general today, teetotalism as a way of life, although limited to a smaller segment of the population, continues to provoke its opposite—alcoholism. A good example is that of Dr. Bob, one of the cofounders of AA. He grew up in a small New England town of "intelligent, hard-working, church-going parents" who frowned upon the use of alcohol as did the other members of the community. Dr. Bob was obliged to attend at least four church services a week and vowed, when old enough to leave home, never to set foot in a church again. This rebellion against such rigid moral standards eventually led him into chronic alcoholism.[14]

Many alcoholics of both sexes have had the same experience. As Kessel and Walton put, "If the parents are rigid in their teetotalism, then the child may in turn become fanatical in his own attitude to drink. Should he also need to express rebellion against his parents he may become as fervent an alcoholic as they were abstinent."[15]

The principal difference regarding women is that a rebellion in the form of drinking has even more serious consequences because the woman's role in a dry fundamentalist culture is more rigidly defined by conventional virtues than it is in a more "open" society.

The Wet Moral Model

From this point of view alcoholics are people who cannot hold their liquor and do not obey the rules of a drinking society. Alcoholism is not a moral failing in itself but rather an unacceptable form of drinking behavior, and alcoholics are guilty of antisocial behavior that often ruins the enjoyment of "good" drinkers. The cause as to why some people act this way is mysterious.

The treatment consists of getting the alcoholic to drink responsibly. It does not consist in getting him to stop altogether, for that would be as antisocial as alcoholism itself. This goal of moderate drinking should be achieved through various rewards and punishments, such as pressure and advice from the family, doctor and friends, changing jobs, exercise and different suggestions on how to drink less or "better." The prognosis is considered good if the right rewards and punishments are found, otherwise the prognosis is gloomy, and if the alcoholic cannot learn to drink like a normal person he may be relegated to the ranks of the impaired. People competent to apply this treatment are all moral members of the drinking society.

Comment

This model of alcoholism is probably the most widespread in our culture. For the person suffering from alcoholism, it is also the most treacherous, for it does not acknowledge the objective possibility that alcohol may in itself be bad for certain individuals. Instead it puts the blame on the drinker, whose inclusion in normal society depends on him doing exactly that which he cannot do, that is, drink normally.

While in the dry moral model the "good" and "bad" alternatives are clearly stated in terms of opposites that apply to everyone, in this model it is not even recognized that such opposites could exist. As a point of departure, drinking is considered as a good thing for everyone. Thus the opposition that exists within actual drinking patterns— addictive versus moderate drinking—is for the most part denied (and along with it the existence of individual differences vis-à-vis alcohol). As a result, those who are adversely affected by alcohol must find fault with themselves alone, rather than question the validity of a social norm that promotes the use of alcohol for everyone. The situation ends up being just as one-sided as in a dry culture where alcohol is banned for everyone. In neither case is the individual taken into consideration.

In such a culture, forms of acceptable drinking may vary from one social group to another. Among the working class, it is important to drink "like a man," which usually means a large quantity. It is all right, even admired, if the drinker gets exuberant and full of bravado as long as he continues to function in other areas of his life. "Tying one on" is part of being virile and a man who can't hold his liquor loses in status among his male friends.

In another class, a man should know his wines and drink like a gentleman. Being drunk is not considered a particular sign of virility. On the contrary, it may reveal a lack of breeding and manly control. But not drinking at all is even more antisocial and reveals a lack of education in the "finer things of life."

No matter what social circle you find yourself in, each will have its own drinking rules. What they have in common is that drinking is good in itself and provides an important element of social cohesion and belonging. Therefore both the nondrinker and the person who drinks "badly," according to the stipulated rules, are looked upon with negative judgments.

For women this picture changes a bit. Even in the drinking society, women can still not drink and feel less pressure than their male counterparts, for whom alcohol and virility are so closely allied. On the other hand, the woman who drinks too much, or wrongly, is judged more critically. While the alcoholic man may be advised to drink less and be reinforced with all sorts of rewards and punishments to help him achieve this (impossible) goal, the alcoholic woman usually finds herself being *only* punished, and more severely than the man. For, whatever her class, she should drink "like a lady" and somehow there seems to be universal agreement on what this means. It means not getting drunk, not causing trouble, not departing from the image of ideal demure womanhood that has prevailed since the Virgin Mary came to represent all respectable womanhood.

It is quite all right for a woman to be a little tipsy, particularly if she is young and attractive, for that goes along with being a harmless and irresponsible sex object. It is not all right, however, to get aggressive or loud or in any way conspicuous because that is not ladylike. The assumption, therefore, under the model of our drinking society, is that although women may drink they do not have the right to get drunk. Somehow the same substance, alcohol, should be controlled or directed by the drinkers so that it provokes effects that correspond to their sex and station in life.

*

In these first three lay models, general ideas of right and wrong prevail. Whether the philosophy be one of Christian piety, moralistic dogma, or correct and incorrect ways of drinking, opinions and feeling judgments hold sway. Since it is these very feeling evaluations which determine so much the roles of men and women, it is not surprising to find that the double standard applies to alcoholism as much, if not more than, other emotionally charged areas such as sexuality and moral values.

As Ruth Maxwell points out in *The Booze Battle,* "There is a greater stigma attached to her disease than to the same disease in her male counterpart. Instead of being considered sick, she is considered wanton and selfish for drinking the way she does."[16] While society finds extenuating circumstances for a man and admits that he might have outside reasons to drink—high-pressure job, monotonous routine, demanding wife, financial problems, etc.—it does not see any such justification for women. Whatever her individual difficulties or responsibilities, her traditional dependence on men and her role as caretaker of his career, his family and his well-being, do not, in the eyes of society, provide the "real" kind of problems that might justify excessive drinking. Therefore, "if she becomes an alcoholic, it is because she has chosen to break a tribal taboo."[17]

I shall return later to this idea of taboo because from an individual and teleological or purposive point of view it contains potentially positive elements. However, from the social, literal point of view the consequences of such a transgression are, for the woman drinker, abandonment and/or punishment. It is a fact that men tend to leave their alcoholic spouses more often than women leave alcoholic husbands. Practically speaking, financial independence and priority of professional activity encourage the husband of the alcoholic to make this decision, as much as the lack, real or presumed, of such financial and psychological independence discourage the wife from leaving her alcoholic husband. The contrast in the general attitude of the public was neatly summed up in a recent London *Times* article in which appeared a random sample of peoples' reactions to the male and female drinker:

About the male alcoholic: "Oh, poor soul. His wife probably drove him to it."

About the woman alcoholic: "Poor husband. He deserves better than that."

Since women drinkers are well aware of this discrepancy and even tend to share the same critical attitude toward themselves, they very often seek secrecy to drink. Thus begins the vicious circle of shame and guilt, making their problem more difficult to treat and to recognize.

The Alcoholics Anonymous Model

The AA model differs from the three preceding in that it addresses only the alcohol problem in itself and does not purport to judge alcoholism from a general cultural standard. It consists of lay people —former alcoholics—whose direct experience of alcoholism gives them a common "expertise" and basis for a common recovery. Therefore the AA groups form a natural bridge between the general population and those who are actually specialized in the field.

First of all, according to AA, alcoholism is defined as an illness which is both progressive and incurable. The causes are threefold, including a physical, emotional and spiritual aspect. But while alcohol is considered poison to the alcoholic in AA, it is not considered so for other people. AA has no opinion about alcohol in society at large. The behavior of the alcoholic—loss of control and compulsive drinking—is symptomatic of his illness. The treatment consists of total abstinence and continuing involvement in AA, a fellowship of recovered alcoholics.

AA members consider themselves to be best qualified to help the alcoholic because they, unlike outsiders (i.e., non-alcoholics), can understand his world and speak his language in a way that supports his efforts at abstinence while challenging his defense mechanisms from an "inside" position. AA does however cooperate with outside authorities. It believes that while it is most competent to deal with the actual drinking problem, it does not necessarily have competence in all the related problems—emotional, spiritual and physical—that enter into the picture of each individual drinker. It is neither a church, a hospital nor a psychological counseling center.

In comparison with the other lay models, the AA concept is the only one with any large-scale success in helping alcoholics. Among the reasons for this is first of all the fact that AA is neither fatalistic nor moralistic. It does not consider that drunks have dropped out of the human race and must be treated as hopeless, if pitiful, cases. Nor does it consider them to be wilfully immoral or antisocial. It considers them sick, and by speaking of an illness it takes away the moral guilt from the individual. It says that alcoholism, like any disease, is something ego-alien, something that strikes from outside and that strikes all sorts of individuals regardless of moral virtue or social standing. One may feel unfortunate in having such an illness but there is no point in wasting energy on self-blame. The important thing is to recognize it and assume responsibility for recovery. It is also important to take responsibility for those debts, both concrete and figurative, that have accumulated during the illness. For just like any severely ill person, the active alcoholic places heavy demands on his environment and he must try to make up for these when he is able.

In brief, the AA model offers some hope, whereas the other lay models only offer a pessimistic prognosis. AA also restores some dignity to the individual by releasing him or her from the status of moral dependent. Lastly, because it respects the right of other people to drink, it frees the alcoholic from the conflict of having to choose between belonging to society and getting sicker or being abstinent at the price of ostracism. Since most alcoholics today are members of drinking cultures, this attitude offers a solution that respects both one's individuality and the need to remain in the collective.

Comment

This is a précis of what AA is as a model in comparison to the others. In a later section, I will go more into the meaning of AA from an archetypal and Jungian point of view, for it forms the basis of my own observations and has provided the context from which I have elaborated my own ideas about alcoholism. But here I would like to ask the same question that was asked of the other models and will be asked in a study of the professional models in the next section: Is the AA model applied in the same way to both men and women?

If the question had been asked in the first years of AA's founding, the answer would have been negative. For AA was founded by men, and while it marked a break from traditional attitudes about alcoholism and new hope for the pioneer members, these were almost exclusively men. It took much longer for women to have the right to be seen in the same light, that is, with an illness, not a moral stigma. In an article entitled "For Men Only?" that appeared in a 25th-anniversary publication of AA, an early woman member writes, "When I attended my first AA meeting on April 11, 1939, I was the only woman alcoholic there." She goes on to say how her psychiatrist had given her up as hopeless after years of intensive private treatment and one year in a sanatorium. At the end he handed her a copy of the book *Alcoholics Anonymous,* saying that the group of men responsible for writing it seemed to have found a way out of their trouble with drinking and that it might help her too. That book gave her hope. She realized that she was not crazy but that she had a drinking problem she could not solve alone.

She found a group in New York and when she spoke openly there about her drinking, she says, "I made the grade. I was accepted as an authentic alcoholic." Still, for a year, despite a newfound sobriety within the group, she suffered from feeling unique and alone. In her doubt, she said to herself:

> At least these men were like me. Or were they? I began to wonder whether this program would work for women. . . . I found it difficult to convince the older members that I wasn't a freak, and to convince the younger members that there *was* such a thing as a woman alcoholic and that I was one. The newer men often found it difficult to conceal their disgust at the idea and more than once, I heard, "If there's one thing I can't stand it's to see a woman drunk." They couldn't believe that women were just as helpless as they were.[18]

She worked hard to attract more women members but it was arduous work, for women themselves brought to bear the same severe judgments on their sisters—or themselves—and continued, as they do today, to hide the problem in a web of deception and fear. In this regard she says:

> We used to hold discussions as to why they couldn't stay sober, couldn't make the program work. Some of the men thought it was because women were more dishonest than men, less direct. "Sneakier" was a word they used. I had to agree that this fit most cases and made

my own task of getting women into AA almost impossible. But I thought I understood the reasons for this—and I still think they are the reasons that keep many women from success in AA today.[19]

The reasons she gives are those already mentioned in previous sections, namely the double standard and image of women who drink as "loose" or "lost." What she also points out is the extent to which this "scarlet letter" was pinned to women *by* women, thus making them their own worst enemies.

Between 1939, when she joined, and 1960, when she wrote her article, things changed. Through her work and that of others like her, women began to come out of the closet and seek help in AA. The attitudes of social discrimination began to change, at least within the AA groups, and women could feel there, if not outside, as free to be sick, rather than "bad," as their male counterparts. "By 1959," she writes, "I thought the corner had been turned, that no one could imagine AA was 'for men only.'"

> Imagine my shock when, 20 years after my solo landing in AA, a woman member in a great Mid-Western city I was visiting told me of several AA groups there that would not receive women as members. As this was true also in many small towns where there was only one group, this meant, in effect, denying AA to women alcoholics.[20]

So, even as late as 1960, women in AA were considered pioneers in a man's world. At that time the membership claimed one woman for every six men, statistics that corresponded more or less to those of the public out-patient clinics. Yet doctors and psychiatrists in private practice claimed then, as they still do, that women alcoholics outnumber the men by far.[21]

Today, some 20 years later, women in AA are not such exceptions and there is probably no group that would attempt to bar them. The statement in the AA preamble that "the only requirement for membership is a desire to stop drinking" has become increasingly true. As AA, originally an all-white male group, has embraced alcoholics of other nationalities and other races, so has it opened its doors to women and people of any sexual identity. While social barriers regarding race, sex and education continue to yield only to the force of law in the outside world, within AA the force of an illness has created a natural democracy.

Even today, however, the official literature of AA reflects the general attitude in society. The alcoholic is still "he," the member of Alanon (relatives of alcoholics) is still mostly "she." This doesn't seem to prevent more and more women from going into AA. But it does show how hard the old images die and how the double standard still prevails in word if not in fact. The reality is simply that

AA is essentially a masculine organization—by its founding and organization and its spiritual program. I think the fact that women do recover within this program reveals something about the meaning of their drinking in the first place. This is one of my main hypotheses, to be explored after a review of professional models of alcoholism.

Professional Models

Among the professional models, I shall explore in particular detail aspects of present-day psychological, analytic and psychiatric points of view (under the one heading Psychological-Analytical). As they exist today, they show fewer successful results but continue to wield more influence in the field than most other forms of treatment. Indeed, the very contrast between the results of a group of "amateurs" such as AA and those of the "experts" is one of the elements that provoked my own interest in writing on the subject, together with the fact that, on the whole, professional models tend to maintain the notion that women alcoholics are not only rarer but somehow more insane, if not more hopeless, than men. This is not always the case, of course. As lay attitudes have evolved, so have professional ones. They reflect and interact on each other.

The Old Medical Model

According to this model, which has probably existed ever since the first drunk consulted a doctor, alcoholism is a serious and eventually fatal disease. Alcoholics generally destroy their bodies and their lives by drinking so much, and this is a kind of immoral behavior that distinguishes their illness from other more "neutral" ones. The cause of their illness is excessive drinking but no one knows why the alcoholic is driven to drink and it seems mostly a question of lack of will power.

Medical treatment of the alcoholic consists first of all in attention to his physical condition, particularly if he is in a toxic state. This demands attention to such problems as dehydration, electrolite imbalance, nutritional deficiency and cirrhosis of the liver. Medication should be given to ease withdrawal symptoms. The treatment should also include warnings and scare techniques aimed at frightening the alcoholic enough about his drinking so he does not undo the work of the physician. These techniques should be reinforced by family members and society who have the right and even duty to police and censure the alcoholic's behavior "for his own good."

The goal of successful treatment is to reintegrate the alcoholic into normal society by getting him to drink "normally." Unfortunately, the prognosis, according to the medical point of view, is poor because the alcoholic will not take care of himself and usually cannot grow up enough to manage responsible drinking. On the contrary, the moment he is released from medical vigilance he tends to undo all the doctor's work by drinking again, excessively and self-destructively. If this happens, then the doctor may become so discouraged at seeing his efforts continually sabotaged that he relegates the alcoholic to the ranks of the hopeless and "impaired."

Comment

This attitude and the treatment that arise from this model are common currency among doctors today, despite the evolution of a new medical model which corresponds better to research in alcoholism over the past 30 years. Although a medical model it is saturated with moral values that do not belong to the generally admitted domain of medicine. Normally, a doctor treats an illness—any illness, from syphilis to war wounds—regardless of the morals or social status of his patients. Medical morality, stemming from the Hippocratic oath, values physical health and life first of all, putting it often at odds with general social morality but preserving thereby a basic and vital counterbalance to the emotionally charged aspects of any pathology.

Within the area of alcoholism, however, this traditionally accepted objectivity gives way to what are basically the attitudes of lay people. Once the immediate medical problems are dealt with, the doctor becomes a representative of ordinary social morality. In trying to get the alcoholic to drink "normally" he mainly reflects the wet moral model of our culture, rather than staying within his own medical ethic which would admit that, in most major illnesses, recovery is desirable but restoration to the former state of health very often impossible. As the authors of "Models of Alcoholism" put it, "The introduction of a nonmedical goal, the restoration of social drinking which then cannot be achieved, has tended to demoralize both the doctors who try and the patients who try and fail."[22]

Furthermore, the pessimistic prognosis of most doctors using this model tends to reflect a layman's fatalism rather than the optimism of a professional in a field which prides itself on advances and victories over hitherto "hopeless" diseases. The subsequent dropping of the patient if he does not make "progress" and labeling him "immoral" go right along with traditional pietistic views maintained by people subscribing to an impaired model. It goes against the medical tradition that holds that a doctor must treat a patient regardless of his condition, and that the moment of crisis is exactly the time to call upon all the resources possible from both patient and surroundings. Instead, the doctor abandons his medical expertise and resorts to moral exhortations.

One of the main reasons for the persistence of this strangely ambivalent, half-medical, half-moral model, is the simple fact that very few medical schools offer any comprehensive studies on alcoholism. Doctors are therefore forced to rely on their expertise for the most obvious physical symptoms, but are not usually equipped with a broader medical understanding about the total disease; unwittingly they fall back into the prejudice of the society in which they participate as ordinary members, with their personal scale of values and quota of complexes.

Because there is so much contamination of general social attitudes in their own reactions, they tend, regarding men and women alcoholics, simply to transfer the double standard from outside their field to within it. Thus women alcoholics are seen as a little bit more immoral, a little bit more hopeless. They are more often given pills to quiet their nerves, sometimes leading to a second addiction. But most often, if they have an alcohol problem, they will hide it from the doctor and he will collude in this denial, for women simply should not be alcoholics and he cannot separate his personal image of womanhood from his medical task to detect and treat an illness.

Fortunately, and very probably because of this ambivalence within the medical establishment itself, another medical model has evolved which is somewhat closer to the traditional confines of medical authority and medical morality, that is, a model which discriminates between its domain and that of other groups.

The New Medical Model

Within this framework, alcoholism is a progressive, often fatal disease. It occurs because alcoholics have a physical intolerance to alcohol that leads to addiction, and most behavior of the alcoholic stems from a need to control the withdrawal symptoms originating from such an addiction. There are also extra-medical factors that contribute to tip the scales and make alcoholics out of people who have this sensitivity to alcohol.

Treatment for the alcoholic includes any necessary medical means to help detoxify and restore health as much as possible. It also includes any means, such as Antabus, which help maintain abstinence from alcohol, for unlike the old medical model, the new one postulates that until an actual cure is discovered, alcoholism can and should be arrested through the only means possible, which is total abstinence. The prognosis for getting over the illness is not very good, for there is as yet no pill or other medical means discovered

that takes away the alcoholic's sensitivity to alcohol. But the prognosis for arresting and living with the illness, as people live with but
are not cured from diabetes, for example, is good. Meanwhile, research goes on and medical science hopes to provide new information and treatments.

Doctors using this model recognize the need to enlist the help of
psychological and social workers in their responsibilities, but they do
not give up treating an alcoholic who has a relapse and "pass the
buck" to the custodians of morals and charitable works.

This model emerged officially in 1956 when the American Medical Association recognized alcoholism as a disease. The shift from
the ambivalent moralistic medical standpoint to one that is more
purely medical, with its emphasis on alcoholism as an illness and
alcoholics as patients, its hope for further cures through research, its
realistic acceptance of the need for abstinence—all these were
brought about in part by pressure from AA and in part from a
general change in attitudes. It certainly has the advantage over the
old model in that it claims within its medical authority to treat the
physical problem but does not claim jurisdiction over other aspects,
thus freeing the alcoholic to seek medical help without fearing the
moral condemnation that society is already all too willing to offer.

Comment

In principle, the attitude toward women alcoholics would be the
same as that toward men drinkers. That is, they each have an illness
and gender makes no difference. But doctors are human beings and
therefore cannot but be influenced by the deeply ingrained prejudices that mark us all, no matter how free or conscious we are of our
complexes, both personal and collective. One doctor I interviewed,
an AA member as well as an enlightened modern physician, could
not help admitting with a sheepish smile, "In spite of all I know
medically about alcoholism and all I know from my own experience
that it is not a moral question, still the one time I saw my wife
drunk I found it much more repulsive in her than in any of my old
alcoholic men drinking partners!"

At least he is aware of his own reactions and in practice he, like
many doctors today, seeks first of all to treat the alcoholic like a sick
person. In hospitals all over Europe and America, for every physician lecturing on the lack of will power and immoral behavior of
alcoholics, there are also others who patiently and repeatedly exert
all their medical know-how to relieve the suffering, promote research and seek the system of support outside of medical authority
that will help maintain the alcoholic's sobriety once he is out of the
hospital.

Old Psychological-Analytic Models

The Traditional Psychoanalytic Model

According to this model, alcoholism is simply the symptom of a deep underlying neurosis, and alcoholics are infantile personalities whose behavior expresses symbolically unconscious conflicts which must be analyzed and traced back to early emotional experiences. If these are elucidated then the patient should be able to give up excessive drinking and achieve a more mature attitude toward life. The only people competent therefore to treat alcoholics are trained analysts or psychologists. But the prognosis is poor, since "alcoholics are usually so infantile that psychotherapy may be needed for a long time before they grow up."[23]

This model dates from the beginning of work with the unconscious in the latter 19th century. In fact, its actual use has been limited, due both to the expense and lack of availability of such expertly trained specialists. Furthermore, when it has been used, it has had a lower success rate in helping alcoholics than any other method, professional or lay. Although many analysts continue to exert their efforts and expertise in one-to-one psychotherapy, the addictions, including alcoholism, do not seem to yield to such techniques and too few therapists have the humility of Jung, who admitted that as far as he was concerned, analysis and therapeutic techniques were simply not effective in dealing with this kind of "possession."

On the other hand, basic psychoanalytic theory has certainly had the most influence on professional approaches to alcoholism. In various forms it is found reflected in almost every psychological or psychiatric approach, as in the following three more or less typical examples. The first two are from psychiatric textbooks in which alcoholism is considered within the realm of other mental illness. The third was developed by psychiatrists specializing in alcoholism.

French Psychiatric Model

According to the French psychiatric text, *Le Manuel de Psychiatrie,* there are two kinds of alcoholism, primary and secondary. *Primary alcoholism* begins very early in the drinking career and is attached to an already severely neurotic personality. The alcoholism may be seen in the form of solitary drinking, loss of control and inability to abstain for more than a short period, but the amount actually drunk may be minimal. *Secondary alcoholism,* on the other hand is characterized by a more biological addiction which only sets in quite a few years after the onset of drinking.

Alcoholism in women, according to this text, is more likely to be of the first kind but it does not repose on what the authors call a "névrose structurée," such as hysteria, phobias or obsessive compulsions. Rather it is the compensation for some kind of failure, a disappointment in love or a revolt against the passive role assigned to a woman in our society. By drinking, a woman asserts her right to be virile and "active" like men. Male alcoholism is described more as an escape:

> Dans l'euphorie de l'ivresse, il réalise, hors des contraintes du monde réel, les désirs et les rêves d'un monde intérieur narcissique et archaique, il vit un réve d'une toute puissance où il peut sans angoisse annihiler l'autre, vécue comme source de conflit.[24] [Trans. in Notes]

This is seen in contrast to female alcoholism: "Pour la femme, l'ivresse est plutôt une compensation d'une conduite d'échec—d'une déception, de la solitude, d'une situation d'abandon."[25] The prognosis, they say, is worse than for men because, although women may more often seek help in the form of psychiatry and doctors, they are essentially more neurotic and therefore more difficult to help.

Interestingly, these descriptions touch upon two of my main ideas, the first concerning alcoholism as a Dionysian explosion and the second concerning alcoholism as a sign of feminine revolt and malaise within constrictive traditional roles. What I would criticize, however, is the fact that the authors seem to think that only men seek escape and illusions of power in intoxication and that, regarding women, they stop short of pursuing their insight about "conduite d'échec" into a more constructive point of view and simply label them "more neurotic."

Anglo-Saxon Psychiatric Model

In Henderson and Gillespie's *Textbook of Psychiatry,* the emphasis in the section on alcoholism is far less purely analytical. They speak about a definition of alcoholism, patterns of alcoholism and signs and development of dependence and treatment, but these remain more descriptive than analytical. Some of the factors they mention with their descriptions are the patterns first proposed by the world-famous expert Jellineck and widely used by people in the helping professions. These consist of "Gamma" alcoholics and "Delta" alcoholics.

Gamma alcoholics are those whose drinking is marked by "compulsiveness and lack of control. They are individuals who cannot drink moderately and are frequently 'drunk, disorganized and incapable.'" The *Delta alcoholic,* on the other hand, is a steady heavy drinker. He is unable to abstain for any length of time but is not disorganized or impulsive and only very late in his drinking career do drunkenness and dependence become characteristic.

The first type corresponds to the French primary alcoholic, one whose tolerance for alcohol is low from the very start, who experiences an obvious change of personality, blackouts and all the follow-up symptoms of remorse, guilt and confusion about the effect alcohol has on them. Though there are exceptions, women tend to drink mostly in this compulsive way. Members of the second group, Delta or secondary alcoholics, are those who can hold their liquor and go on for years, never drunk but never quite sober. More men tend to fall into this category and they tend to succumb to alcoholism only when the actual physical addiction sets in.

Whatever the actual type, the reasons for alcoholism, according to Henderson and Gillespie, are found in a combination of social circumstances and a vulnerable personality. Childhood environment is most often marked by such disturbances as parental quarreling and/ or separation, and deprivation of basic emotional security. Later on, peer pressure, exposure to alcohol, personal mishaps and psychological problems will add to the reasons for excessive drinking. The signs of growing dependence are a mental preoccupation with drinking; secret drinking; drinking before social occasions; drinking to cope with tension, with work or with life; deterioration of work and social life; guilt, remorse and paranoia; and finally blackouts.

The treatment includes abstinence, then a psychological study of the individual's life and personality and the cultivation of healthy hobbies to replace the drinking habits. Aversion therapy is recommended for the "less intelligent patient who may be inaccessible to dynamic psychotherapy."[26] AA is also recommended because of its "outstanding success and in spite of the fact that it fosters an overdependence on emotional and religious factors that hinder the development of true individual maturity."

Having given this rather backhanded compliment to AA, the authors conclude, regarding the therapeutic methods they propose, that in fact the results of psychotherapy are not very convincing. They end the section on alcoholism with the pessimistic statement that the prognosis for an alcoholic is generally poor, and state that "We are unable to form any conclusive opinion on the value of psychotherapeutic methods in the treatment of alcoholism."[27]

Regarding women, there is no special point of view here simply because, among the different types mentioned, the alcoholic is still always "he." The only mention of women is "his wife," who needs to be understanding and supportive if the man is to get well.

Specialist's Model

In the textbooks cited above, alcoholism takes up only a small section among more elaborate ones devoted to the neuroses and psychoses. It is described and some effort made at proposing treatment, but the authors themselves admit to being unsatisfied with the results and tacitly admit that alcoholism simply doesn't come into the same category of mental disturbances that are so authoritatively discussed in other parts of the book. Perhaps because of this impasse experienced by general psychiatry when confronted with all addictions, more and more specialists have appeared, both within and without the psychiatric domain.

The example here is taken from the book *Alcoholism*, referred to in chapter one, written by psychiatrists who made alcoholism their speciality and therefore claim to be rather more versed in their subject than their generalist colleagues. Like Henderson and Gillespie, Kessel and Walton speak of patterns of alcoholism, causes and treatment, but they go into more detail. They also attempt to delineate more precisely the kinds of personality apt to be alcoholic.[28]

As an introduction, they place alcohol first in a biological-cultural context, pointing out that alcohol acts as a depressant, not just on mood, which can be the first thing to be affected, but more important, on the part of the brain which controls socially-adapted behavior. As this control is the "product of the highest mental processes," it is also the first to be impaired. Under the influence of alcohol, therefore, the individual experiences a release of normal restraints and inhibitions. In Western culture this might mean an increase in acting out aggressive or sexual impulses that are normally censured. The excessive drinker therefore often drinks as a gesture of rebellion against his society.

Another factor they point to is the impact of the loss of traditions and cultural values that lead to greater individual tensions and disarray. A study of alcoholism among Italians in Italy and among Italians in America tends to confirm this. It was found that in Italy about 60% of the men and only 10% of the women drank too much occasionally or frequently. In the United States, however, the figure rises to 84% for the men and 50% for the women. Clearly, uprootedness from the security of the collective container contributes to alcoholism—as it does to most other problems.

Going from cultural patterns to individual cases, the authors describe five different personality types that are susceptible to alcoholism:

The Immature Personality. These individuals are especially mother-bound men, marked by a need for approval and admiration and dependence on parental support long after normal childhood. Thus they are caught in an incestuous relationship that cannot be satisfied and have recourse to drink in order to find fantasies of fulfilment that the real world denies them.

The Self-Indulgent Personality. These are men whose overprotective parents deprived them of personal achievement and fostered a need for instant gratification. They live by the pleasure principle, seeking only to reduce frustration and discomfort. For them, "drink is a celebration. Sybarites, they isolate the pleasurable part of reality. When drinking, they dim the lights, play music and even at times costume themselves. They act like voluptuaries."[29]

The Sexually Disturbed Drinker. These men have sexual problems and they fall into three categories: 1) Those who have too little sex drive and drink because their wives express dissatisfaction and recrimination; 2) Those who fear sex as dirty and cannot relate to women. They are victims of romantic obsessions they cannot live and drink to attempt to release their inhibitions; 3) Lastly, there are what the authors call the deviants—the homosexuals, the sadists, the fetishists, the voyeurs. They drink to relieve shame at such perverse practices or to achieve normal behavior.

The Self-Punitive Personality. These are men who have repressed feelings of hostility since childhood and as a result live under constant tension. Alcohol provides an "irresponsible and unconscious way of expressing inner hostility."[30]

The Stressed Personality. These people come under the basic neurotic model. They are perfectionists, hard on themselves, living in continual stress regarding outside or inner conflicts. Alcohol provides relief and may even ward off the actual neurosis.

Not content with the simple primary/secondary or Gamma/Delta divisions, the authors go on to elaborate on the ways that these different personalities might express their alcoholism. Here they find six types, including the *Unsuspecting Alcoholic,* the *Regular and Restrained Alcoholic,* the *Compulsive Alcoholic,* the *Neurotic Alcoholic,* the *Symptomatic Alcoholic* and the *Bout Drinker* or *Dipsomaniac.* How these types correspond to the previous categories is not stated.

There is no mention of women in these personality sketches and the assumption is definitely that the alcoholic is a man. However, within descriptions of drinking patterns the authors do add a little note on women. They mention that women, due to social convention, are mostly secret drinkers and home drinkers who do not get drunk but cannot abstain. "They often make a pathetic attempt each evening to hide evidence of drinking, both upon themselves and in the neglect of their homes before their husbands return from work."

Aside from the condescending tone, many women who have been very drunk both at home and at work, with and without husbands to clean up for, would take issue with this blanket statement.

In a later part of their book, discussing the alcoholic family, they mention the fact that women alcoholics are more often left by their husbands than vice versa and that their marriages are usually less stable than those of men alcoholics. The reasons they give are the usual ones, namely that men's drinking is more socially acceptable, that women are more financially dependent, etc. But to these general reasons, they cannot resist adding that "women alcoholics have in the main more disturbed personalities than their male counterparts."[31]

Once the various personalities and drinking patterns have been described, the writers go on to mention the social and cultural factors of incitement, opportunity and example. In the personal-psychological area, they speak of fixation at early developmental stages, childhood patterns carried over into adulthood, regression in time of stress and faulty ego development. In particular, they say that oral fixation is common to all alcoholics; that is, regardless of personality, all are prone to possessiveness, clinging and infantile impulses leading to excessive dependence on others, either overtly or covertly. The reasons for their infantile characteristics would be found either in deprivation of basic maternal security—which leads to a constant search for assuagement—or in an overindulgent mother and inconsistent father, the mixture of which creates exaggerated needs for affection, protection and care. All alcoholics, they conclude, suffered severe emotional trauma or deprivation in their childhood, mostly in the form of parental quarreling, absence of a parent, basic insecurity and inconsistency.

Comment

Most of the above explanations would be confirmed and agreed with by most psychotherapists. One could go on to review all the material produced by analysts and therapists and find much the same theory regarding oral fixation, lack of ego development and infantile impulses and dependence. One could also find other descriptions of drinking patterns and personalities, with slight variations in treatment proposed. In good journalistic style they all attempt, within the expertise of their psychological training, to answer the questions: Who? What? Why? When? Where? and How? and then to formulate a treatment based on these findings.

I chose to describe the approach of Kessel and Walton because it is such a good example of the good, bad and ambivalent that comprise the contribution of psychological models to alcoholism. The categories of drinkers and drinking patterns are genuinely interesting in themselves—certainly as well-observed and differentiated as any others—and they could be useful in diagnosing and treating various kinds of alcoholics. Yet understanding has not cured many alcoholics, as witness the statements by so many who say they tried individual therapy, learned about themselves and yet continued to drink.

Unfortunately, too, the authors' language is riddled with such moralistic, puritanical, holier-than-thou values regarding the weakness and inferiority and perversion of alcoholics that it is difficult to believe the writers are professionals whose role is to help and not to judge. As representative of the old psychological-analytic models, they fall into the same trap as those doctors who still work with the old medical model. That is, they approach alcoholism with their professional training but quickly get caught in the wider social prejudices that reflect more the lay view of impaired and immoral beings than of a professional view of suffering patients. With this unspoken set of values it is not surprising that their attitude to women alcoholics is either more judgmental or just plain superficial.

New Psychological Models

Not all analytic or therapeutic attitudes are so discouraging. Today, more and more professionals are approaching alcoholism from a point of view that admits and seeks other supports outside of the purely psychological one-to-one treatment. It is generally admitted that the best solution is a combination of personal therapy, family discussion and maintenance through a support group such as AA. Many of the findings of those professionals who have specialized in addiction and alcoholism are, in fact, much closer to the AA and Jungian attitudes, for they emphasize the importance of spirit as a primary aspect of alcoholism and eros (relationship) as a prime factor in the cure.

One such individual is David A. Stewart who wrote *Thirst for Freedom,* an account of his experience with alcoholics and his conclusions about approach and treatment. He does have a certain model in relation to definition, personality, patterns and treatment. It combines, however, traditional psychological views with more openness to the unclassifiable human factors and feeling values that mark the AA approach to alcoholics and the Jungian approach to the psyche.

In brief, Stewart says that all addictions are characterized by exposure to the addicting substance, distress at withdrawal and taking of a drug to relieve this distress. Like AA, he defines alcoholism as a threefold illness, but instead of mental, physical and spiritual, he says medical, psychological and social. He also postulates the possibility of a biochemical defect that provokes an allergic reaction in alcoholics, unlike normal drinkers. This has yet to be proven and most professionals refuse the hypothesis, stating flatly that, contrary to the stand of AA, alcoholism is not a disease per se. Stewart remains open to the possibility, making him one of those who subscribe to the optimistic outlook of the new medical model. He emphasizes social customs and morals as primary influences in the development of alcoholism, and he thinks that treatment should include a combination of abstinence, therapy and maintenance in the form of AA or other organizations.

Stewart's conclusions are not altogether revolutionary. They coincide largely with much that has already been presented from psychiatric models and most people using updated psychological criteria would agree with Stewart. However, besides his less moralistic attitude and ability to describe without hiding behind defensive professional jargon, there are two main features to his presentation that set him apart from the professional mainstream. One is that he dares to use terms such as "spiritual craving," and even dares to say that, after all the reasons are understood and dealt with, "addiction remains a mystery for the same reason that religion is a mystery."[32] Thus he comes very close to Jung's view, as expressed in his letter to Bill Wilson, cofounder of AA, that the craving for alcohol is "the equivalent, on a low level, of the spiritual thirst of our being for wholeness; expressed in medieval language: the union with God."[33]

The second element that sets his book apart is the section on women. Unlike many of his professional peers, he does not dismiss the problem by citing women's greater mental disturbance or social immorality. On the contrary, he devotes a large section to theoretical and practical aspects of female alcoholism. In a later section I will be referring to his ideas both on alcoholism as a spiritual problem and on women alcoholics in particular.

*

Whatever their particular training, most professionals agree on certain main points: that alcoholism comes from a combination of personal and environmental factors plus exposure to the liquor; that the personal causes include repression of unacceptable feelings, escape from painful ones and creation of pleasant ones; that treatment consists first of all of abstinence and then of various social and psychological supports. The differences are ones of emphasis. Some persevere in trying, despite the negative results and evidence, to cure alcoholism through one-to-one therapy, maintaining that insight will bring an end to the compulsion. Others, more and more common today, admit that therapy alone is generally impotent. Some still put the emphasis, despite professional language and careful elaboration of categories, on the immorality of the alcoholic. Others try to maintain strictly objective mechanistic standpoints and still others are more open to the area of mystery and "soul" or spirit that transcends their purely professional training. The examples given here do not include all the possibilities, but are fairly representative of the mainstream approaches.

The Family Interaction Model

This last model for alcoholism is the most recent. It holds that alcoholism is a kind of family interaction in which one person plays the alcoholic and the others play complementary roles such as the martyred wife, the neglected children, etc. The behavior of the alcoholic never stems from strictly personal or psychological motivations but must always be seen as one in a series of moves in an on-going family "game." As these games are "circular and self-reinforcing," it makes no sense to ask about the precise play. In general, certain family traits are transmitted from one generation to the next and the roles predetermined so that their distribution is more or less accidental. The only people qualified to deal with such a constellation and the games involved are therapists trained in family counseling and "game playing." The prognosis for recovery is good if such therapy is used but poor otherwise.[34]

Comment

This model owes its origin largely to the work of Claude Steiner, author of *Games Alcoholics Play.* Practically speaking, it has had little effect because it has the same handicaps as the old psychological-analytic models: it is expensive and requires very specialized personnel who are by no means available wherever there are alcoholics. But its theoretical impact, like that of psychoanalysis, has far outreached its practical application. It has opened the doors to more interest in the total family situation, recognizing that those who live with alcoholics are apt to be as disturbed as the alcoholic and that changes in one must bring about changes in the other.

This conclusion is not entirely new. Alanon, the group for relatives of alcoholics in AA, was formed out of just this realization. Jung, too, repeatedly emphasized that any individual neurosis or unconscious conflict contaminated other people as well. He pointed out that those who did not deal with their own shadows inevitably forced others to deal with it or to act it out. As early as 1912 he stated how much the unconscious attitudes of parents influenced and even determined the destiny of their children.[35] He was one of the first to emphasize the influence of one generation upon the next and how a family "curse," whether it be in the form of a complex or alcoholism, was apt to be carried on until one individual was able to confront it and arrest it.

Therefore, the actual content of Steiner's contribution adds nothing totally original. But his bestseller style, breezy and glib, and his catchy techniques do present the alcoholism problem in a form more accessible to the general public than other more "serious" professional approaches. One can wince at his glibness and at the "cruise director" jargon he employs to describe kinds of alcoholics and "moves" in the game. Yet one is still obliged to admit that these very labels, such as "Drunk and Proud," "Lush" and "Wino" present just as true a picture of drinkers as the most expert but humorless descriptions proposed by the psychiatric texts. Many insights about alcoholics, for example the need for permission not to drink and the so-called family "scripts" that they must live out as part of the family theater, are actually quite apt.

Unfortunately, the family interaction model remains more valuable for its theoretical and popular impact than for its practical use. Although Steiner sought to take alcoholism out of the hands of the professionals and to create a sort of "everyman's version of understanding and coping with alcoholics," he wound up contradicting his own goal when it came to means. In the end, according to his idea, everyone can play and even know *what* they are playing, but only a very few specially trained individuals can referee the game. And what's the use of playing if there's no one to keep score?

Regarding women, Steiner makes no obvious value judgments. He both admits the existence of women drinkers and suggests special needs they might have relating to the cause and cure of their excessive drinking. His description of them, however, suffers from the same defects that the rest of his model suffers from. That is, it is too schematic and too facile. He claims that women make up all of the category he calls "Lushes" and this arises from the lack of closeness and "strokes" from their husbands. Men, on the other hand, he says, are more in the "Drunk and Proud" category and drink to express feelings of aggression and omnipotence. His portraits of these two categories are quite convincing and it is true that many women and men drinkers fit the labels. But many do not. There are "Lush" men as well as "Drunk and Proud" women, not to speak of many other types he simply ignores in his desire to simplify for the masses. Furthermore, behind his labels lurk the usual assumptions of women as totally dependent on men, drinking only in relation to husbands and somehow more inferior as alcoholics than men. After all, a "Lush," whatever the definition, evokes a far less dignified picture than does a "Drunk and Proud" drinker.

Conclusion

Altogether the models presented above cover the general attitudes and ideas about alcoholism in men and women that prevail today. None is absolutely pure. Most draw on others to reinforce their own point of view. For instance, the old medical model uses the morality of the impaired or wet moral model when its own expertise comes to an impasse; the new medical model uses the resources of AA; the psychological-analytic models use AA, the new medical model and psychological premises belonging to traditional psychoanalytic theory.

What all the models have in common is a certain attitude toward women alcoholics. As separate entities they are mostly ignored. When their existence is recognized, they are considered more impaired, more immoral or sicker than the male. While in the worst of cases, a man still has the right to be called an alcoholic and thereby benefits at the very least from a certain pity, a woman who drinks excessively seems more often to be considered bad than sick. Her sex counts against her even more than her problem. The exception to this opinion is found in AA, although as was seen this has not always been the case. There are also exceptions among professionals (e.g. David Stewart) who have made it their business to study the problem more openly.

Still, much remains to be explored regarding women drinkers. Although many of the same psychological mechanisms are applicable to women as well as to men, many are not and there are few new insights in current literature regarding the particular aspects of female alcoholism. This is what I shall attempt to provide in later chapters. For while cure or recovery has been greatly increased through such methods as those of AA, and although causes and types of alcoholism have been greatly elucidated through psychological research, the *meaning* of alcoholism remains to be explored in depth. It is in this area that analytical psychology has something to contribute.

2

Jungian Concepts and Alcoholism

What Jung Said about Alcoholism

There are few specific references to alcohol and alcoholism in Jung's writings. During his early years as a psychiatrist he published an article called "On Manic Mood Disorder" in which he presented and described four cases whose symptoms also included alcoholism. This symptom, however, he considered secondary to the basic "psychic degeneracy" of such individuals. The main problem was considered by him to be a hypomanic state, not yet psychotic, not real mania, but characterized by emotional lability, flight of ideas, distractibility and overactivity and restlessness. From these, in turn, resulted such secondary symptoms as "exaggerated self-importance, megalomania ideas, alcoholism, and other moral defects."[36]

What prevented these individuals from being morally insane was the fact that they were not feeble-minded. In all cases, Jung noted, the intelligence was good in contrast to the outward conduct of life which was "extraordinarily inept." He saw no lack of ethical feeling either, but rather a basic emotional abnormality that led to pleasure-seeking, based on "an excessively sanguine temperament which serves as too mercurial a basis for the intellectual process and fails to give it the necessary continuity of feeling-tone."[37] The only difference between his descriptions of the two men and one woman lies in the emphasis Jung put on the woman's hypersensitivity to outside stimuli, her depressive reactions to censure and strange preference for the company of "inferiors" such as servants, rather than the company of her social peers.

This conforms to the general pattern, then as now, of women being more defined by outside social expectations than men and appearing even stranger when they seek, consciously or not, to come into contact with unlived "shadow" elements.

Reading Jung's description today, it is difficult to know how much should be ascribed to the diagnosis "manic mood disorder" and how much to the actual drinking problem. One could speculate that in fact the emotional lability, although existing from childhood, was maintained and worsened by alcohol. And that if the alcoholic problem had been solved for good and not just temporarily, as in the case of these patients during their stay in the clinic, the other emotional abnormalities would also have been corrected or at least dealt with in a less self-destructive manner.

43

The point here is that many active alcoholics could be described in almost the exact words that Jung uses. While drinking they are irresponsible, restless, unreliable, emotionally labile, full of inflated ideas and other moral defects frowned upon by society. Yet these same people, upon recovery and abstinence from alcohol, are seen to change not only from their alcoholic days but also from their pre-alcoholic personalities which were already emotionally labile. It is as if the process of becoming sober not only arrests the drinking but transforms the drinker.

Such transformations do take place, and not infrequently, in AA for example. But at the time of this early study of Jung's, he was still very much within the orbit of early 20th-century psychiatry with its descriptions and half-veiled judgments on what constituted inferiority in the individual. His great contributions, which concerned the importance of psychic plurality as opposed to monolithic ego consciousness, the healing power of the unconscious, and the value of the individual as opposed to the collective, were yet to come.

There is another reference to alcoholism in *Psychological Types,* written some years after Jung had broken with traditional psychiatry, as well as with Freud, and had undertaken his own exploration into the unconscious. Here alcoholism is mentioned in the general description of types at the end of the book, where Jung states that it is one of the dangers for the extraverted types. Because they depend on and overadapt to outside reality, a split between conscious and unconscious is created in which the subjective (or introverted) elements are repressed. These subjective elements may include any and all affects, needs and feelings, infantile or archaic demands, which when suppressed for cultural reasons "easily lead to a neurosis or to the abuse of narcotics such as alcohol, morphine, cocaine, etc. In more extreme cases the split ends in suicide."[38]

Later, however, Jung qualifies this possibility as one likely to happen only to men. For men, he says, are stronger on the outside due to their masculine logic and objectivity but they are more vulnerable within, due to the unconsciousness of their feelings and anima-related reactions. Therefore, Jung says, a man is more likely to be "a victim of impulses from the unconscious, taking the form of alcoholism and other vices."[39] Women, on the other hand, he says, are softer on the outside and therefore more victims of outside circumstances but not so liable to despair and inner torment, due to the fact that their unconscious soul, or animus, is masculine and has the same traits of objectivity and toughness that a man displays outwardly.[40]

These comments on alcoholism are a long way from the psychic degeneracy theories of Jung's early writings. Now the emphasis is more on intrapsychic regulation and compensatory mechanisms between persona and shadow, individual and collective. But the comment on women's lesser vulnerability to inner demons recalls Victorian attitudes, if not medieval ones, in which theologians could not agree on whether women even had souls. Today, at any rate, the development of feminist consciousness and the struggle for value in a man's world has given them the "right" to the same ills, impulses from the unconscious, alcoholism and other vices formerly considered the prerogative of men.

Returning to Jung, however, we find it does not help to look for specific references to alcoholism. Rather one must look to the archetypal themes he explored throughout his life, patterns that in Jung's view serve as points of reference for *any* type of behavior.

Perhaps the most important in terms of alcoholism are the opposing themes of Apollonian and Dionysian consciousness. Jung perceived that the Dionysian element of "divine intoxication" was an important human experience that required some expression within ritualistic confines, and he observed that the Christian Church had gradually rid itself of such "pagan" manifestations, leaving room only for "mourning, earnestness, severity, and well-tempered spiritual joy."[41] These insights of his are crucial to an understanding of alcoholism. If, as Jung says, possession is part of the religious experience and intoxication is "the most direct and dangerous form of possession,"[42] then by excluding the more exuberant, irrational Dionysian elements from its ritual, the Church turns Dionysos into the Devil who "throws the gates of hell wide open."[43] Instead of divine intoxication, we end up with addiction and alcoholism, possessions by the dark side of the neglected archetype. This theme will later be explored and seen within the lives of specific women.

First, however, we shall look at Jung's general ideas on psychic development and disturbance and AA's philosophy regarding recovery from alcoholism, compared with the theoretical models previously described.

Critique of Theoretical Models

Moralistic versus Moral

The first three models, reflections of lay attitudes toward alcoholism, are basically moralistic, that is, according to whatever specific collective standards they represent, they propose a kind of behavior that should be adhered to by all and which the alcoholic violates with his or her immoral drinking pattern. Many people today object to these moral judgments, and with good reason, for if the alcoholic is condemned a priori as a sinner and a fallen member of society, then there is little chance for recovery. In fact, one of the important contributions of the AA movement was to counteract this powerful moralistic aura that had always surrounded alcoholism and to have it accepted as a genuine illness in which the patient was responsible for recovery but not for being ill in the first place—just the opposite of the usual attitude in which the patient, particularly the woman, was considered bad to *be* alcoholic, but too irresponsible to recover.

It should be noted that in AA there is a pre-eminently moral—as opposed to moralistic—emphasis, both in the wording of the basic Twelve Steps and in the atmosphere of weekly meetings. For example, members are encouraged to live without acting out their anger or resentments, to review their drinking lives and make amends to people they may have harmed, and to continue carrying the AA message to other alcoholics, regardless of time or place. These and other AA principles belong to a way of life that could only be called moral. Yet there is a difference between the public morality, or *moralism,* which condemns the alcoholic and the AA morality which supports him or her.

This difference seems to parallel Jung's differentiation between collective and individual moral standards. It is a subject he repeatedly returns to throughout his work and his insights expose the fallacy of applying a general morality to any individual problem. In brief, he stresses the fact that each individual must face his own dark side, his shadow, and participate actively in the conflict between good and evil, dark and light. Collective codes, while necessary, do not apply to any particular individual. Worse, they can be, and often are, used as escapes from personal effort.[44] The question is not *what* is done but *how.* Thus nondrinkers or "good" drinkers may be judging the alcoholic out of facile conventional standards and even hiding behind an attitude that satisfies public standards but is not related to the individual psyche.

According to Jung, a sense of conscience and moral right is engrained in human beings and must be followed if there is to be any genuine individuation.[45] The alcoholic's immorality in relation to collective standards, therefore, is less relevant than his violation of his own psychic possibilities. In neither case is there a real choice, and choice, for Jung, is the only criterion for genuine morality. Therefore, when AA stresses the need for moral principles in recovering from alcoholism it is, in fact, applying in a group what Jung sought to apply to individual situations; that is, the idea of facing the shadow—which manifests as the dark side of drinking— and then going beyond it, recognizing the need for certain limits that every civilized being needs in order not to fall into chaos and destructiveness. As Jung so unequivocally states in his letter to Bill Wilson:

> I am strongly convinced that the evil principle prevailing in this world leads the unrecognized spiritual need into perdition if it is not counteracted either by real religious insight or the protective wall of human community. An ordinary man, not protected by an action from above and isolated in society, cannot resist the power of evil, which is called very aptly the Devil.[46]

Of the new kind of morality that comes into being after one accepts the shadow, Jung remarked:

> When a man knows himself, then he will know the mistake that is in himself and therefore he has to face it. When you accept yourself, then the world can accept you. . . .
> It takes a very peculiar kind of experience to make people believe in anything like a spiritual law. It is exactly this experience which would prove the existence of an entirely different type of living, though in itself it is not necessarily spiritual.[47]

This describes very well the experience of those alcoholics whose recovery has led to a discovery and acceptance of certain basic laws, whether they be called moral or spiritual, that are both more individual and more universal than conventional codes.

Materialism versus Meaning

With professional models the problem involves not an interpretation of morality, but rather the issue of inner as opposed to outer meaning. In contrast to medical models, the general Jungian viewpoint is that a purely physical approach is too materialistic to account for or to cure the total human being. As Jung put it in "Basic Postulates of Analytical Psychology," the new creed of the age is based on matter rather than spirit. With its hormones, enzymes, instincts and drives, the body has come to be seen as the creator and determining factor of the psyche, instead of matter (i.e., body) being conditioned by the soul, as had previously been believed.[48]

This materialistic tendency did not begin only in the 19th century. It began to take over as a *Weltanschauung* when the "vertical" consciousness that culminated in the Gothic period yielded to the "horizontal" consciousness of the Renaissance and the Reformation. It was then that the ego became the center of all, expanding its territorial conquests outward, into overseas colonies and scientific experiments, instead of aspiring upward toward the divine. In a phrase, "Other-worldliness [was] converted into matter-of-factness."[49]

The reality, as Jung goes on to say, is that matter and spirit coexist, both as opposites and as realities in themselves, to be explained in terms of their own origins and then to be reconciled so that both the natural man and the spiritual man can live. Ideally, they come together in the concept of *psyche,* which gives birth both to physical and spiritual awareness.

Unfortunately, whereas matter was denied and martyred by the teachings of Christianity until the Renaissance, now the pendulum has swung the other way. Medicine may see a cure for alcoholism and even isolate an enzyme that separates alcoholic drinkers from normal drinkers, yet many questions remain unanswered. What about the spirit of alcohol that is expressed in the possession of intoxication? And the spirit in the rebirth experienced by alcoholics who come back from their "dark night of the soul"? It may indeed involve a biochemical reaction, but one cannot help but look for the psychic element as well, for "truth that appeals to the testimony of the senses may satisfy reason but it offers nothing that stirs our feelings and expresses them by giving a meaning to human life."[50]

Similar criticism could be leveled at the psychological and psychoanalytical theories reviewed in chapter one. But in so far as they mention the influence of the parents and infantile attachments, Jung would probably agree. He was already writing in 1903 that what influences a child most are the unconscious, personal affective states of the parents and teachers. Twenty-seven years later, he reiterated that the undifferentiated ego state of the child manifests as *participation mystique,* a condition of unconscious identity with the parents. This means that what affects the parents' unconscious will affect the child's unconscious and that their attitudes and lives will have far more influence on the child's personality than their words or pedagogic exhortations.[51]

This agrees with the findings of professionals: children of alcoholics do often become alcoholic, but the children of teetotallers may also become alcoholic—the former under the influence of the visible example, the latter under the influence of the parents' unacknowledged shadow and unlived lives, the lives they "shirked ... by means of a pious lie."[52]

As for the infantile traits that professionals emphasize so much regarding alcoholics, Jung had earlier stressed that in *all* psychological problems, "the misfortune is always too strong an attachment to the parents, so that the child remains imprisoned in its infantile relationships."[53] Thus one could say that Jung's basic theory of neurosis as a failure of adaptation in which reality is falsified through earlier, inappropriate modes of adaptation, has been taken up and simply elaborated on for alcoholics.

Yet despite moralism, medical research and psychological insight, alcoholism continues to spread and no magic cure has been found. Certainly it is not that the work of pastors and doctors, psychologists, friends and family is useless or in vain. It is just that it isn't enough, for it is almost always reductive, as opposed to synthetic or purposive. It is necessary to look forward as well as backward. If the knowledge of causes could cure, then neither neuroses nor addiction would continue to bother mankind. Causal factors are certainly relevant but are only part of a human being's story. The other part is comprised of meaning—and that cannot be obtained from universities, churches or libraries, for these only move the head and not the heart. The alcoholic has a thirst that is more than physical, one that causal explanations do little to allay.

Classification versus Understanding

To conclude this section I would like to cite some of James Hillman's comments from his book *Suicide and the Soul.* He broaches the problem of models when introducing his subject, and there are striking similarities between the things he found were said about suicide and what I have found said about alcoholism.

For example, regarding the common trend toward classification, he quotes a well-known expert as saying, "The first major task of any thoroughgoing scientific study of suicide is the development of a taxonomy or classification of types of suicides."[54] Compare this to Kessel and Waltons' words: "Psychiatrists must carry out a careful process of differentiation to determine the category in which a particular alcoholic belongs."[55] In both areas it is the outside approach that holds sway, and the trap lies in turning the total person into a mere type and case.

Some clue as to why there is this relentless need for classifying and diagnosing in both alcoholism and suicide is glimpsed in Hillman's statement about suicide in society: "The law has found it criminal, religion calls it a sin, and society turns away from it. It has long been the habit to hush it up or excuse it by insanity, as if it were the primary anti-social aberration."[56] How closely this resembles Siegler and Osmand's introduction to "Models of Alcoholism," where they speak of alcoholism as a "disputed ailment" which provokes such a combination of contradictory attitudes in attempts to master or avoid it.

Furthermore, what Hillman says about existing models for suicide is equally true for those concerning alcoholism: that they are *all* basically inadequate because they leave out the psyche and are therefore bound to defining and speaking only in terms of collectively tolerated standards, such as defined by the medical Establishment, the Law, Church or Society. As all of these depend on essentially rational values, there is no room for other than causal factors. With them one may find reaction patterns and discover mechanisms, but one loses the soul.[57]

Spiritual meaning is not to be found in rational, reductive classifications and causes—particularly the meaning of such socially inadmissible behavior as killing oneself or drinking oneself into a stupor. If, in fact, alcoholism is a kind of slow suicide, then it isn't surprising that collective attitudes are similar in both, especially in our Western society which more than most fears death and with it all signs of the irrational that threaten life as defined and determined by the conscious, responsible ego. Like suicide, drunkenness offers freedom from an ego tyranny that plagues us all; it offers a kind of oblivion, a way out of the constraints of our petty self-consciousness. And, like suicide, alcoholism expresses a refusal of life in the conventional, collective understanding of it. But if it cannot be understood through ego standards of conscious rational modes, how can alcoholism be understood, if at all, and what does it say about an individual's experience of life?

Understanding, according to Hillman, is not based solely on theoretical criteria but on "sympathy, an intimate knowledge, on participation."[58] This intimacy and participation are what I have experienced with alcoholics in two contexts: Alcoholics Anonymous groups where I have been an occasional guest for several years, and in the analytical setting where I have worked with women analysands who were alcoholics, both active and recovered. In later chapters I will be drawing on material from both these contexts. AA provides the basic framework, the closed vessel in which both the illness and the cure are to be observed. But within the AA setting there is no attempt to explain or grasp the meaning of excessive drinking or to highlight the differences between men and women alcoholics. This is not its purpose, which remains essentially one of staying sober and helping other alcoholics to achieve sobriety. Therefore, AA corresponds to the alchemical *laboratorium* or laboratory where the work was actively engaged in and the *prima materia*, the raw material, worked upon. But in alchemy there was a second and complementary aspect to the work—the *oratorium* or library where theory was developed from the findings in the *laboratorium*.

What I shall do, therefore, is to regard the AA groups as my laboratory and empirically develop ideas that might add to an understanding of the action undertaken. In effect, I will be moving from the alchemical *laboratorium* to the *oratorium*. The tools I shall use will be mainly those of Jungian psychology. To a certain extent this will include a study of causal factors and Jung's ideas on parental complexes. But as the primary emphasis in other studies of alcoholism is generally on these more reductive aspects, I would like to focus on aspects less often explored, in particular the archetypal patterns that Jung illuminated. These will include Dionysos and Apollo, already mentioned; the wounded healer motif personified by Aesklepios that gives a certain dimension to the apparently simple methods of Alcoholics Anonymous; and a search for feminine archetypal patterns, also taken from Greek mythology, that help to place the woman alcoholic within her own myth and meaning.

James Hillman expresses it well when he writes on the purpose of studying the archetypal in order to understand the human:

> The deeper a psychology can go with its understanding, i.e., into universal inner meanings expressed by the archetypal speech of mythical "tellings," the more scientifically accurate it is on the one hand and the more soul it has on the other.[59]

3

Archetypal Patterns in Alcoholism

The Dionysian and the Apollonian

What kind of gods were Dionysos and Apollo? What does it mean when we speak of the Dionysian and the Apollonian, and why are the two gods—and concepts—so often seen as conflicting opposites?

Apollo

Apollo was third in the Olympian religion, ranked only after his half-sister Athena and his father Zeus. He was born of Zeus and Leto, herself a goddess, granddaughter of Ouranos and Gaia, the original world parents. The brilliance and glory of Apollo were evidenced from his birth on the island of Delos, where Leto came to deliver her son far from the jealousy of Zeus' official spouse, Hera. It is said that at this time, on the humble rock that made up the island, the foundations, the rivers and even the trees turned to gold, that swans sang and flew above in symmetrical circles, that fragrance filled the air and that even Hera lost her anger at the bidding of Zeus.[60]

The coming of the young Apollo brought light and harmony to preside over, enrichen and order the natural world. Suckled not at his mother's breast, he was given nectar and ambrosia, the food that was due to him as a son of Zeus and that marked him as great among the gods. Once he had tasted of this divine food, "no mortal bonds could restrain him." Already as an infant, he slew the dragonness Delphyne (whose name derives from "womb") in order to make the Delphic cave his own for his oracles. Psychologically, this feat represents the victory of solar consciousness over the undifferentiated, devouring feminine.

But it was also Apollo who sent his sister Artemis to slay his unfaithful mortal lover Koronis, and then sent pestilence to devastate the land of her family; and Apollo who pursued and carried off the women he desired, regardless of their desire.

Apollo is first and foremost the spokesman and representative of his father Zeus, patriarchal sovereign of Olympus. As Apollo himself announced at his birth, "In my oracles I shall reveal to men the inexorable will of Zeus." Spokesman of the patriarchal order from the distant heights of Olympus, he is unforgiving when crossed and yet "a great lord over mortals and immortals." All the gods rise when he enters and if he hurts with arrows, he soothes with his lyre, thus earning the descriptions "Leader of the Muses" and "He who brings Nature into Harmony."[61]

Thus Apollo has come to represent the solar consciousness of a detached ego, civilizing and moderating influences, ideal forms, high aims, harmony in nature and the arts, a point of view that is detached, distant and objective. Positive from the point of view of the development of consciousness and freedom from the irrationality of the instincts and the suffocating power of the primal feminine, he is nevertheless destructive in his one-sided masculine values that can sear and scorch to death the new life and imaginative stirrings that need darkness and moisture for growth.

Dionysos

Apollo's half-brother Dionysos, on the other hand, comes from another world. He is not a "pure" god, born to Olympus, unreachable and above the mortal sphere. Rather, through his mortal mother Semele, who conceived him, and his father Zeus, who gave birth to him from his thigh after Semele was consumed by the blaze of her lover's overwhelming divinity, Dionysos partakes of both heaven and earth. Many sources say that he was also an "outsider," a stranger to Greece who arrived from the East, from Thrace or Phrygia. Walter Otto disagrees with this, proposing that Dionysos existed long before the story existed in Greece of his entering from outside. Nonetheless, figuratively he is an outsider, raised to Olympus only late in his career around the 5th century B.C., but always remaining antithetical, a stranger to the norms of the official, structured Olympian cult.[62]

Half-man, half-god, product of two realms, he carries within himself the duality that his origin implies. Unlike Apollo, Dionysos was not given god's food at his birth but suckled by nurses in the wild forest. Some stories say that his wet-nurse was Hipta, a name given to the Anatolian great goddess who was also the chief divinity of the legendary Amazons. Thus Dionysos from the beginning is not a representative of the patriarchal order like his half-brother, but a god of women, suckled by and attended by women, accompanied by women in his wanderings and even to his death, danced awake once again by women who usher in the ever-repeating rebirth of the god who must die in order to live again. For both life and death belong to the earthy, chthonic realm of Dionysos and he, in the form of innocent child killed by Hera's Titans, or martyred man, victim of manly heroes who despise and fear his androgynous ambiguity, must partake in his own archetypal destiny.

Not only is Dionysos a god of women in fact, but he himself is called "Feminine One" and is said to be bisexual, thus reflecting in gender as well his pervasive duality. In every description of Dionysos one is struck by the multiplicity of his names and attributes and appearances. While Apollo represents Olympian Zeus, the one source of wisdom and counsel and might, and speaks from the distance of detached consciousness, Dionysos incarnates all the contradictory forces and forms of life and death on Mother Earth. He is called Deliverer, Loosener, Delight of Mortals, God of Many Joys, Benefactor, Bestial and Wild One, Eater of Raw Flesh, Renderer, Merciless, Savage Destructor.[63]

There is no god so praised, or so vilified, as Dionysos, god of ecstasy, god of joy, god of madness and sorrow as well, god of extremes and paradoxes. As Otto says so poetically, "All earthly powers are united in the god: the generating, nourishing, intoxication and rapture: life-giving inexhaustibility and the tearing pain, the deathly pallor, the speechless night of having ... been."[64] Opposed to Apollo and the civilizing, regulating, harmonizing influence of the third Olympian deity, the mere presence of Dionysos "stripped mortals of all their conventions, of everything that made them civilized and hurled them into life which is intoxicated by death at those moments when it glows with its greatest vitality."[65]

The Dionysian-Apollonian Opposition

We have already seen some illustrations of the Dionysian-Apollonian differences. We see Apollo for example in the present-day struggle for equality between men and women and the redefinition of social and sexual roles. For, ironically, it is women themselves who, in seeking to change their dependent status, end up simply usurping the men, defining themselves according to Apollonian standards of technical and intellectual excellence rather than seek new archetypal feminine models from among those that have been neglected in favor of the old traditional models of wife (Hera), housekeeper (Hestia), mother (Demeter).

Even the women who choose to remain faithful to the traditional modes are, as we have seen, more and more impinged upon in their domains by the all-pervasive voice of Apollo who speaks for "Father Right" and masculine values through travestied versions of his oracles—the press, radio and TV.

Secondly, it is the Apollonian criteria that prevail when stages of addiction are divided into 54, and even in the descriptions of reasons why people drink and the personality traits that are common to alcoholics. Orderliness and generalities are Apollonian; they satisfy the intellect's need for structure and clarity.

Lastly, we see Apollo in the models described and the judgments brought to bear upon alcoholics in general and women alcoholics in particular, in the search for forms to contain, for distance to observe from, for diagnoses to differentiate and defend those who are on the "right" side of the norm and those who are not. All these are indicative of the Apollonian. The fact that women alcoholics are somehow considered more sick is a verdict that descends from the Olympian heights, the place of "Father Right" where woman's place is defined in terms of man's and her irrationality seen in terms of aberration.

Objectivity and order and clarity are not bad in themselves. There is surely a need, in any problem, to establish some kind of order and to have a certain conscious point of view. The negative side only enters in when the Apollonian claims for itself the *only* right, a monopoly on the truth, as it has come to do in our overintellectualized, egoistic society.

Yet Apollo himself insisted on reverence to others than himself, "by inner necessity to supplement the scope of his own domain."[66] He could step aside to acknowledge the rights of these other archetypal entities, and in particular he acknowledged Dionysos as his opposite but complementary brother. That the two gods, the one celestial, the other terrestrial, could and did coexist side by side is confirmed in the archaeological findings at Delphi, the place of Apollo's temple and his oracle, the place where he was, therefore, the most numinous and powerful. Within this very sanctuary it appears that there was also a grove of Dionysos, god of woods and the wild.

Forest and temple, nature and civilization, side by side, as if to state how inseparable the two really are. Furthermore, Apollo shared the Delphic festival year with Dionysos, and one finds the pediments upon which rests his temple inscribed on one side with Apollo and the Muses, on the other with Dionysos and the Thyriads, a group of his women followers.[67]

This coexistence has not entirely disappeared in contemporary society. Despite the apparent predominance of Apollonian conceptualization and even the abuse of it in many contexts, the presence of Dionysos can be detected nearby when the viewer simply changes focus.

Dionysos is there, for instance, in the contemporary collective confusion about sexual roles. For the more that Apollonian consciousness attempts to discover and locate exactly what gender means and where it originates, the more confusion ensues. Whether one takes a stand for traditional roles or for equal rights or for homosexuality or for androgyny, for hormones or for environment, whatever the position it is only one, and Dionysos will reappear with some contradictory evidence—reminder of the underlying paradox of life, that no one-sided point of view, however progressive, suffices to explain or to contain all.

Dionysos is there too in the very multiplicity of the models and ideas and attitudes toward alcoholism. While Apollo would seek one structure, one harmonious totality to embrace the problem, Dionysos comes with his disrupting, fragmenting influence. Attempts to regulate and coordinate turn into a Tower of Babel in which different schools vie with each other. The hubris of subscribing to science as a unified objective language is revealed in all its relativity. While trying to describe alcoholism as a manifestation of Dionysos, from a distance and from above, the describers themselves get caught in his irrational multiplicity.

In studies of alcoholism, however, despite the upsetting emotional effect of Dionysos on those who would remain cool and detached, most of the descriptions, and especially the values, of experts and nonexperts alike are Apollonian ones; Dionysos appears mainly as the problem, the illness—"Crazy, weak, inferior, sick." These same epithets that Greek heroes gave to Dionysos are implicit in references to alcoholics, women especially. Perhaps even more than in most areas of our culture, in alcoholism the archetypes are set at odds with each other, fixed in irreconcilable opposition—sobriety versus intoxication—rather than integrated in a complementary relationship.

We see this not only in the way alcoholism is described with models and formulas but in the actual content of the words used. Thus the reasons given for drinking—to ease tension, to dull the pain of duty or personal relations, to ease fatigue and boredom, etc.—all these describe an escape from constricting Olympian standards. They describe Dionysos as the Loosener, the Ecstatic and Untamed, one who brings relief as his father Zeus decreed he would when he told his mistress Semele, the mother of Dionysos, that she was blessed, "for you will give birth to intense joy for gods and men, for you have conceived a son who brings forgetfulness to the sorrows of mortals."[68] + WAS BURNED TO DEATH FOR CONCEIVING HIM

Dionysos may bring an annoying end to the security and safety valued by conventional order. But in exchange he evokes a flow of life. Where he is, according to the myth, rocks burst and water rushes out, chains are burst from prisons, barriers are lifted and inspiration replaces routine. Everything that has been locked up is released and "earth flows with milk, with wine, with nectar of bees." One of the greatest miracles was on Parnassus where the women danced to awaken him as the divine child, and on his awakening the grape vine blossomed and ripened in a day.

But Dionysian miracles belong to the god, not to mortals, so that when a person identifies with the god and attempts to loosen all constraints in a day or an hour with alcohol, Dionysos may show his darker side. Then he becomes a god of madness and destruction, one form of which may be alcoholism. How this manifests and what it may express about the lives of individual alcoholics, especially women, is the subject of the next two sections.

The Female Drinker

The first page of the brochure "AA for the Woman" presents a list of questions that situate and illustrate very precisely the drinking life of the woman alcoholic. They are as follows:

1. Do you buy liquor at different places so no one will know how much you purchase?
2. Do you hide the empties and dispose of them secretly?
3. Do you plan in advance to "reward" yourself with a little drinking bout after you've worked hard in the house?
4. Are you often permissive with your children because you feel guilty about the way you behaved when you were drinking?
5. Do you have "blackouts," periods about which you remember nothing?
6. Do you ever phone the hostess of a party the next day and ask if you hurt anyone's feelings or made a fool of yourself?
7. Do you take an extra drink or two before leaving for a party when you know liquor will be served there?
8. Do you feel wittier or more charming when drinking?
9. Do you feel panicky when faced with nondrinking days, such as a visit to relatives?
10. Do you invent social occasions for drinking, such as inviting friends for lunch, cocktails or dinner?
11. When others are present, do you avoid reading articles or seeing movies or TV shows about women alcoholics, but read and watch when no one is around?
12. Do you ever carry liquor in your purse?
13. Do you become defensive when someone mentions your drinking?
14. Do you drink when under pressure or after an argument?
15. Do you drive even though you've been drinking, but feel certain you are in complete control of yourself?

From the beginning it is clear that these questions are addressed to and describe *women* drinkers. Unlike the lists of symptoms and steps mentioned in official textbooks that describe from afar the

male alcoholic's progressive advance into aberrant pathological behavior vis-à-vis his wife, work and adult responsibilities, this list of
questions offers an "inside" viewpoint. It does not concern itself with
what the drinker looks like, but with what she *feels* like and what
she *does*. It portrays a relationship that the drinker has to the bottle.
This is vital, for example, in the case of well-heeled suburban imbi-
bers who *look* very different from their sisters in sordid slums or
bars but who share with them an *attitude* toward alcohol.

And this attitude, as the questions manage to convey, is one of
devotion to the bottle, that is, to Dionysos. A woman who answers
affirmatively to many or most of these questions is a woman who,
above all, is *busy* with alcohol. She is busy buying it, hiding it,
finding excuses to drink it and having to find excuses after she
drinks it. She is acting like a *maenad,* one of the female followers of
Dionysos—his muses, his protectors, his adorers. They nursed him at
birth, followed him into the wilds and awoke him from his sleep-
death when he disappeared into the underworld. It fell to them to
organize and perform the cult practices and ecstatic dances in service
of the god, and his passion became their own. With this god women
surpassed themselves. The *bacchantes* and *maenads,* following Dionysos as the Great Loosener, could partake in his liberating powers.[69]

This feeling of being *more than*—more powerful in both charm
and physical possibilities—we see reflected in the questions "Do you
feel wittier or more charming when drinking?" and "Do you drive
even though you've been drinking but feel certain you are in complete control of yourself?" We see the *devotion* reflected in the
questions on obtaining alcohol and defending the occasions for
drinking it. Lastly, all the questions taken together point to ways of
acting that are not in accord with accepted standards. The devotion
to Dionysos implies a revolt against the opposite, the too-rigid Apollonian social conventionality. The hiding and planning and ingen-
ious inventions to find time and reasons for Dionysos, are all taken
away from the world of Apollo, a world in which women are ladies
at parties, devoted, attentive mothers with their children and responsible, competent housewives whose work is all in the service of the
family world where she should be Hestia and Hera but certainly not
a *maenad.*

Psychologically, one could say that excessive drinking for a
woman is above all a kind of *antipersona* way to act. If, as Jung says,
the persona is "a functional complex that comes into existence for
reasons of adaptation,"[70] an outer attitude concerned with relationship to outer objects, then it is a kind of mask that is needed for life
in the collective but it is not at all synonymous with individuality.
Esther Harding goes even further in emphasizing this last point and

her description is especially pertinent to women. The persona, she says, is a result of socialization and training, "whose object is to teach [the child] how to adapt to society, what is permissible or not, what will produce love and acceptance and what will be frowned upon or punished."[71] Whatever is perceived by the ego to be socially unacceptable will be repressed into the unconscious and become part of the shadow, the alter ego or other person within.[72]

Persona and shadow are complexes. We speak of "persona-identification" to describe an individual who lives too much according to a social image or role and too little in accordance with his or her more individual, if perhaps less socially adapted, nature. For each person, these complexes will be a little different, formed according not only to social criteria but the influence of family values as well as individual tendencies and talents.

But there is also a collective persona and a collective shadow. In Western culture, the collective feminine persona corresponds pretty much to the archetypal patterns personified by Hera, Hestia and Demeter. In practical terms these correspond to particular orientations: children (Demeter), kitchen (Hestia) and church (Hera—spouse, therefore Lady of Official Spiritual Values, which are those of an institutionalized, patriarchal Church). These archetypal patterns reflect images of woman seen through an Olympian perspective where Zeus reigns and Apollo gives utterance to his father's will. Women who drink too much shatter these stereotypes, these persona masks they are supposed to wear; they enter the world of Apollo's opposite, the world of Dionysos, where instincts and irrationality of the earthy, chthonic realm replace the civilization and clarity of the Olympian.

Women alcoholics are perhaps a modern phenomenon in that women in former times were far less susceptible to this "male affliction," but they are not original in their susceptibility to the call of Dionysos. On the contrary, they have sisters and models within the legend of Dionysos and not only in the general, undifferentiated picture of the *maenads, thyriads* and other feminine groups that surrounded this god of women. They have predecessors in the daughters of royalty, of Proteus and Minyos, these daughters who were driven mad by the god when they attempted to resist Dionysos in fidelity to their Hera personas. Hera, Queen of Heaven, detests, more than any other divinity, the wild actions of the god and his female band because they make a mockery of her entire realm, the established bonds of marital duty and domestic custom.[73]

The image of the woman leaving the role allotted to her by an Olympian interpretation of woman's place is therefore an archetypal one, especially relevant today when feminine being and behavior

have been reduced to a basic three out of the six Olympian goddesses, and roles of women since the 19th century have been so
strictly limited and devalued by development of the very technology
which was to free them, as well as men, from menial and humiliat-
ing tasks. To understand the woman alcoholic, therefore, one may
begin by referring back to the original myth of Dionysos which, as
Otto relates,

> tells again and again how his fury ripped [women] loose from their
> peaceful domesticity, from the humdrum orderly activities of their
> daily lives, for the purpose of making them into dancers in the wilder-
> ness and the loneliness of the mountains where they find him and
> rage through the night as members of his revel rout. . . . We find again
> the picture of the woman who runs away from domestic life, the
> realm of Hera and marital duty and of the handiwork of Athena to
> rush with hair dishevelled to the choral dances of Dionysos.[74]

In legend it sounds picturesque and even romantic, these women
with flowing hair and loosened limbs. In actuality, a woman possessed by the alcohol aspect of Dionysos may in certain moments of
intoxication feel just so free and ecstatic as she lets herself go and
breaks the conventional bonds of her usual roles. But intoxication is
not just ecstasy, and possession by the god can be one of the worst
experiences as well.

The following two stories illustrate such a possession and they
show as well the influence of Apollonian values that both precede
and follow the descent into alcoholism, values that, when too one-
sided and stereotyped, provoke their opposite but when more bal-
anced may bring about a healing process.

Two Women's Stories

The last chapter looks in detail at alcoholic women I have interviewed and known personally. The material here, meanwhile, will
give a general perspective on the type of woman who "chooses"
alcoholism as a solution to conflict, rather than some other social,
neurotic or even psychotic "solution."

The two stories are taken verbatim, albeit abridged, from the
brochure "AA for the Woman." I do not know these women. I know
nothing of their lives beyond what they tell of themselves, which
relates almost exclusively to their alcoholism, its course and cure.
These accounts thus serve to illustrate in a concentrated form the
interplay of collective, archetypal patterns more than purely personal
psychological elements would. My comments after each story will
focus on the Apollonian-Dionysian tension, pointing out how it is
expressed and how it is resolved.

A Housewife

"My mother died when I was 12 years old and I used to think that my life would have been different if she had lived. However, I now know more about the illness of alcoholism and I do believe that my problem was already a part of me, even at that time. I was full of feelings of inferiority and extremely shy. My father did his best in raising me and my two sisters, but naturally he didn't know too much about girls. Still, he kept the family together until I went to college.

"I can remember the overwhelming fear that gripped me as my father got ready to leave me at that college. I wept and begged him not to make me stay, to let me come home. I knew I was not going to be able to cope with getting to know all those people. And I didn't. I was a misfit from the beginning and felt like one. So my years at college were not the gay time so many people recall but years of hurt feelings, rejection and anxiety.

"Although I had never been popular, with many dates (I was never a pretty girl), I did finally get married. My husband was a very handsome man, and I used to be smugly amused when people would say to me, 'How did you ever get such an attractive man?' Now that I was married I thought I would lose my fears and no longer be so anxious with people. Unfortunately, this was not the case. Every time I had to meet business acquaintances or other friends of my husband, I would find myself tongue-tied—unless I had a drink. I had learned at college that a drink or two made it possible for me to communicate. And three drinks made me forget that I wasn't pretty!

"Eventually we had children, and they meant everything to me. Yet I would awake horror-stricken to realize that I had been driving the car around the countryside in a blackout, the children with me.

"Then my husband became very ill. Lonely and frightened, I felt the need to drink, even though the children—and now my husband— were dependent upon me. Much later, when I came to AA, I was easily able to accept the thought of God's grace, for I could look back at those many times when my children were playing unattended while I slept off the morning's drinking.

"We moved to a small town and I hoped that a brand-new social circle would solve the problem. But during that time I was very resentful toward my in-laws with whom we were living. Eventually my resentments—and my frustration at the fact that we had to live with these people—brought me back to the rationalization that perhaps things would be easier if 'we' had a drink before dinner. It seemed to assert 'our' independence of them in some way. I can guarantee that one way not to endear yourself to your mother-in-law is to get drunk publicly in a small community. I often did.

"One night, feeling lonely, I went to a bar a few miles from our house, leaving my son, who was then about eleven, in charge of his sisters. One of the men in the bar offered to drive my car home, but I argumentatively told him I was quite capable of handling it. Driving back, I crept along the winding roads until I was about a hundred yards from our driveway. I speeded up and crashed. . . . I thought I had reached the depths at that point.

"I've learned in AA that we cannot get sober for anyone else, but only for ourselves. However, <u>I do believe that there has to be some motivating factor that makes us want to get sober</u>, and I am sure that for me the motivating factor was my children. I will never forget my little girl's fourth birthday party. I promised her a lovely party. I spent so long planning for it. When the day came, the mothers brought their children, took one look at me—and stayed for the party. I was so drunk that they could not leave their children alone with me.

"This breaking of promises to my children finally brought me to the realization that I could no longer live with myself, and so I turned to AA for help. Like most of us, I had no idea of what I would find when I came to AA. I was full of the usual misconceptions about it. I thought that alcoholics were only Bowery characters. At my first meeting I was surprised to meet people who I knew were church members.

"More important, when I first walked into an AA meeting, I had that wonderful feeling of belonging. Talking with the people there, I discovered that I was not a freak. I was not the only person in the world who had done the kind of things I had done, had hurt the people I loved most. I was grateful to learn that I was suffering from an illness. I had been afraid that I might be going out of my mind.

"During my first few years in AA, I had trouble getting to meetings regularly. The children were small, and it was not always easy to find someone to come and sit with them. Nonetheless, I fell in love with AA from the very first meeting and somehow knew that through this program I was going to find the answers.

"In time, through AA's Twelve Steps, I realized that if I would accept the love that was being offered to me so freely, and try to share it with others, I could learn through AA to be comfortable with people. To me this was a wonderful step forward. And it led to one of the greatest gifts that AA has given me: no longer to be afraid. My life had always been dominated by fear; fear of people, of situations, of my own inadequacies. In AA I learned to have faith and so to live without fear.

"My life has not all been easy since I have been sober, but at least I have been able to cope with the problems that have come along. And I feel that my children, too, have received a tremendous gift in being brought up in this AA way of life: the Steps, acceptance, living one day at a time. May I never forget to be grateful for all that has been given to me."

Comment

This woman's story is that of a "typical" housewife. She corresponds to the image of the "pathetic" or "neurotic" female alcoholic depicted by textbooks: a woman who drinks out of boredom and/or lack of moral fiber, and who betrays her sex as wife and mother in exhibiting such unfeminine, unmotherly behavior when under the influence. Middle-class homemakers like this who tipple their way into addictive drinking are legion in the offices of doctors and psychiatrists, who with all good intentions tend to prescribe tranquilizers and hobbies. The picture is practically so mundane that no one bothers to look behind the scene. But the archetypes are just as present in this apparently banal portrait as in the more dramatic ones.

First, we see that as a woman she felt inferior from the beginning. Having lost her mother, feeling rejected by her father, not popular at school, not pretty as a girl, she had little going for her in a society that places so much emphasis on women as socially attractive creatures. Because she herself doesn't seem to have been able to imagine herself as more than a potential wife and mother, she placed her total existence in the classic Olympian order where men come first and she could exist as wife-Hera, mother-Demeter and housekeeper-Hestia.

But in her case, perhaps because she had always felt like a misfit, the doors of Olympia cracked and Dionysos, the "Outsider," came in to disrupt this perfect façade. Very early on he came as "Loosener," making her feel less tongue-tied and, as the god who loved women, "made me forget that I wasn't pretty." But since she was so insecure in her Olympian roles and could probably only don them as persona masks and not as real ego identities, Dionysos rapidly made more inroads into her world until she soon felt the need and compulsion to drink all the time, just to keep going, to keep up the roles as well as to repose from them.

From Loosener and God of Joy, Dionysos became god of unleashed emotions and disrupter of civilized harmony, as we see in her anger toward her duties as wife, and her unladylike behavior when she alienated her relatives by getting drunk in public. This is also seen in the incident of going to a bar by herself and then

64   **Archetypal Patterns in Alcoholism**

driving home and having an accident, full of Dionysian aggression and assurance, despite her lack of control.

The turning point came when she was closest to incarnating the most feared and negative aspect of the *maenads,* the dark side of the Mothers. For just as the *maenads* nursed and protected the baby Dionysos, so they also, in their bloodthirsty madness, could destroy life, thus reflecting the "wild spirit of opposites" that the god himself incarnates. Carried away by Dionysian ecstasy, their dances may become death orgies in which the child is torn to pieces. While this remains within the supernatural context, mortals are not free either from such horrors, as is shown by the madness Dionysos sent to the daughters of Proteus, who then set upon their own sons.[75]

So we see that even within the average middle-class life of an ordinary woman, this *maenad*like madness can strike; the neglect, if not abuse, of her children may often be part of an alcoholic woman's Dionysian behavior. For the woman in question it was this—the spoiled birthday party and the breaking of promises to her children —that was the turning point. She then realized that she was in trouble and could no longer live with herself. It was as if the positive, nurturing aspect of the *maenad* overcame the negative side when the latter became too threatening to ignore. At that moment she called for help and went to AA where, from being an isolated misfit, she gained a "wonderful feeling of belonging," an outsider with other outsiders.

This sense of belonging is a common and key experience of nearly all alcoholics who become members of AA. It seems to signify the end of a negative kind of individualism and their integration into the collective. But it is a collective that is based not on conventional persona norms—the very factors that often provoked drinking in the first place—but on a deeper bond of common suffering and understanding.

Indeed, there is a Dionysian element in the warmth, the liberating atmosphere of AA that allows people to share and to be themselves —and a Dionysian element in the very fact that it is a group. AA therefore compensates to some extent for the more Apollonian atmosphere of a society that values, above all, intellectual strength and individualistic self-reliance.

But Apollo is not absent from AA. On the contrary, in AA, unlike society at large, Apollo and Dionysos come into some sort of reconciliation. If the group offers a Dionysian context for expression of feelings and for security and containment in the Great Mother who lies behind this god, the AA program brings in the Apollonian aspect as well. As the woman tells it, not only does she feel good and accepted but she *learns* that alcoholism is a threefold illness, she _works_ the Twelve Steps, living one day at a time, she _copes_ with problems that overwhelmed her before.

Thus the elements of clarity, conscious striving and spiritual values, positive aspects of the Apollonian, can come in to balance the more emotional and Dionysian ones. Unlike the one-sided adherence to patriarchal, Olympian standards that leads to just as one-sided a devotion to Dionysian values, membership in AA seems for this woman, and many others, to allow for a healing of the individual through a reconciliation of opposites.

A Singer

"At the age of 16, I started out on my own to pursue a career. I wasn't exactly sure what career, but I knew that I wanted to make a success of my life, and marriage was not my cup of tea. I got a job as a secretary in a large firm.

"In my job I did well, getting raises, but I wasn't content with secretarial work so I began entering contests: talent contests, singing, playing instruments; competitions for College Queen, Miss This or That. Through winning these contests, I was offered a career singing with big bands on the road, traveling all over the country—something I had always wanted to do.

"All very glamorous! By the third day of traveling, I found I was having a terrible time sleeping. The musicians' answer was a game they played on the bus: 'Pass the Bottle.' This helped me to sleep, but it had one drawback: it made me so sick that they had to stop the bus for me every five minutes.

"Later, I started missing the bus because I was drinking. I went into hospitals because I was drinking. I was unable to perform because I was drinking. I went to church, and I prayed not to drink like that any more. Funny, I never prayed to stop drinking: I prayed not to get drunk.

"Soon the attempted suicides began. I took overdoses of pills, made weak attempts at slicing my wrists. I jumped out of cars. I woke up in a hospital in a straitjacket, screaming, 'God, why did You let me live? If You're letting me live, why don't You show me how?'

"From that day on, I hated God. I hated myself. I hated everybody. I felt the loneliness of the alcoholic though I worked with people: I traveled in the bus with them. But they saw my behavior at all times, and no one wanted to have anything to do with me. There was no place I could hide. I decided to go to New York, believing that if I settled down, got an apartment of my own, had a life of my own, perhaps my drinking would get better.

"Always lucky with my work, I got a job, singing in one of the best hotels in New York, rented an apartment, and 'settled down,' promising myself I would not drink on the job. Opening-night parties were the only occasions when I did. Even then I seemed to drink differently from other people. Strange. The one thing I wanted was to be like everyone else, yet I always felt different.

"One night I caused a scene and was told that if I got drunk again I would be fired. I was no longer a 'ladylike' drunk. I had a favorite bar and would head there immediately after work. Somewhere along the line I would lose my salary, probably giving it out as a tip. I had developed a 'big-shot' complex. Toward the end of my drinking, I wasn't welcome in bars. So I began to bring bottles home. I was afraid to drink anywhere else, I was afraid of the phone, of a knock at the door, of the mail, of everything. I was filled with fear.

"One day I woke up after just another drinking bout, not as bad as many that I had had. But I was so disgusted and filled with self-hatred that I decided to kill myself. Decided it, this time, with a fairly sober mind. First I had to go to work. That way, there would be no phone calls checking on me, and I would be undisturbed the whole night to do what I had to do. I went to my dressing room and tried to put on my make-up, with tears streaming down my face and my hands shaking. The make-up kept running, and I couldn't put my lipstick on, and I couldn't put my eye make-up on, and I had had it.

"Before I'd finished dressing for the performance, I took the phone-book and looked up Alcoholics Anonymous. I called, and a man answered, and I started crying hysterically, 'I'm not an alcoholic. I don't know why I'm calling you. I'm insane and they should put me away. I'm not on the Bowery. I haven't lost my job. I'm only 27. I can't be an alcoholic!'

"The man on the other end of the phone said, 'Tell me, has alcohol ever interfered with your life?' Those few words seemed to say, 'I know what you mean. I understand.' It's funny—I stopped crying right then.

"The next day AA women came to see me. I was sick and shaking and filled with self-hatred, and when these well-dressed women came in, all I kept thinking was: Could I ever be like that? They told me that alcoholism was an illness. I knew how I had tried to drink normally and it had never worked and I could never understand why. Now I did. I had an illness, called alcoholism.

"I was thrilled to know that I wasn't insane, thrilled to go to meetings and to meet people. I heard their laughter, true and clean, most of it at themselves. I had thought I could never laugh again, but the loneliness went away and I learned to laugh. Spiritually, I have gone back to my church (or to God) and I find that the AA philosophy helps me to understand my church all over again. Mentally, with the Twelve Steps and slogans and the Serenity Prayer, I have found peace. I don't hate anymore and I am no longer an emotional hemophiliac. I'm not afraid of yesterday, and I'm not afraid of tomorrow. I live today.

"I worked in nightclubs for five years after my recovery and have only recently stopped singing. Now I'm married to a wonderful man and happier than I'd ever thought possible. Yes, marriage *is* my cup of tea."

Comment

In many ways, the singer's story differs from that of the housewife. For one, she breaks with the traditional feminine role from very early on, wanting to pursue a career and knowing that "marriage was not my cup of tea." So, instead of accepting the usual position of women vis-à-vis men, she, ambitious and adventurous, determines instead to be *like* one. She lives the masculine values of Apollo—work, ambition, competition, glamour—rather than living in their shadow and adhering to men as a subordinate. Early in her career, however, this one-sided choice must have started to affect her for she became insomniac—a surfeit of consciousness that would be the ultimate in Apollonian possession!

It was then, as could be expected, that Dionysos entered the picture and offered alcohol as a way out of her tension. In a way he was already there, since she had chosen singing as a career and the world of theater and performing arts are among the rare *accepted* versions of the Dionysian in our culture. But music also belongs to Apollo, since it was attributed to one of his Muses. Music, therefore, can be harmony or dissonance, control or eruption, Apollonian or Dionysian. When it is confounded with ambition and is a way to be accepted and admired by the collective, it expresses much more an Apollonian mentality, as in this case. Ironically, Dionysos only stepped in with a vengeance when her musical career began to bring more problems than satisfaction. Then alcohol became not only a way out of her sleeplessness but quickly took over her life.

From her clear, directed, professional aspirations that made no concessions to any other aspects of life, she found herself smitten by just as total a manifestation of the other side: failure, suicide attempts, hospitalizations, dissolution and dependence, blackouts and a kind of alcoholic madness, all these expressing the mystery of Dionysos who insists on his place and will take it by force if repressed.

For this woman the turning point came at a moment of both figurative and literal dissolution when, unable to go on, she had decided to kill herself and then went for a "last" performance into her dressing-room where "I tried to put on my make-up, with tears streaming down my face and my hands shaking. The make-up kept running, and I couldn't put my lipstick on, and I couldn't put my eye make-up on, and I had had it."

Here the image reminds us once again of the multiplicity and paradoxes of Dionysos. Yes, he was a god of madness and of death, of alcohol in its joyous as well as in its destructive aspect, but he was also a god of moisture, the element that creates and maintains life. Otto points out that "the cults and myths are as explicit as they can be about the fact that Dionysos comes out of the water and returns to it and that he has his place of refuge and home in the watery depths."[76] The singer who wept evoked this beneficent aspect of Dionysos and in her tears the madness itself and the ego resistance both dissolved for a moment, leading her to pick up the phone and call for help.

When she shortly thereafter joined AA, she indeed found a "refuge and home" within the group. She found the same end to loneliness and a feeling of belonging as did the alcoholic housewife. She also found a new way of relating to Apollo—no longer only through ambition and collective standards of perfection but in a more genuine spiritual sense, helped by an actual return to the church and the use of the Steps and slogans and Serenity Prayer. She says she is no longer an "emotional hemophiliac," which would have been the result of too much conscious rationalism compensated by an uncontrolled overflow of emotions—perhaps the only way for the tension of opposites to be resolved. Consciously she aspired to Olympian heights; unconsciously she was pulled into Dionysian chaos.

This woman too, within AA, was able to experience the Dionysian and the Apollonian in a complementary way. She even married as well. Whether this marriage was a regression into roles she formerly rejected is a possibility but an unlikely one, for in her AA involvement a certain "religious" attitude protects her from absoluteness or one-sidedness.

This religious attitude, as well as the feeling of finally belonging, are elements that one finds in the testimonies of almost all AA members, no matter what their different backgrounds and drinking stories. We have seen them expressed already by the housewife whose story and personality seem quite different from that of the singer. Yet they had a common experience of a too rigid form of individual expression based mostly on Olympian, masculine ideals—whether they attempted to live these ideals as equals or as predestined subordinates. Then they both were struck by the opposite compensatory Dionysian archetype that, in turn, became one-sided and destructive. But only through this destructive side did they eventually come into AA which became for them a way to the resolution of the opposites. Their alcoholism was a kind of *felix culpa,* a "fortunate crime" that led to a new awareness, a transformation from persona-identification to a degree of individuality.

According to Jung, it is *only* when there is a collapse of the collectively adapted persona, and when the conscious mind loses its leadership, that the individuality which has its source in the deep layers of the collective unconscious can begin to emerge.[77] In many, and perhaps most cases, he says, this does not and should not happen—particularly as long as the adaptation to outer reality is the primary task and takes up most energy. But when the problem of inner adaptation comes to the fore, as it does in almost all cases of neurosis, then the unconscious begins to exert a "strange, irresistible attraction" and "a powerful influence on the conscious direction of life."[78] At such times analysis can help to both precipitate and contain the personal collapse necessary to further development. But life often provokes other ways of forcing collapse, of which alcoholism may be one. Then Dionysos becomes the agent of the collective unconscious that may, if the destructive dark side is overcome, bring about a more individual consciousness.

Bill Wilson, cofounder of AA, coined the expression "hitting bottom," meaning that each individual must reach his or her own low point before being able to ask for help or want to change. In 1936 he wrote, "The alcoholic must hit bottom and his ego must be deflated totally before he is ready for AA."[79] These words are echoed by Jung: "Only those people who really can touch bottom can be truly human."[80]

Thus the alcoholic woman who goes down far enough to lose at least her persona and identification with collective models has the possibility, if her illness leads her to AA or a similar "refuge," of re-emerging as more of a human being. Once defeated, she can learn to accept the dark side of life, the "ugly man" (or woman...) that Jung so often referred to, and that "to love oneself one needs to hold communion with people... to see that you are just the same, that all suffer from the same problem."[81]

Aesklepios, Apollo and Alcoholics Anonymous

Now, besides a general kind of religious experience and feeling of belonging, a combination of Dionysos and Apollo, what is it that AA offers to the women alcoholics who find help there and just how does it "cure" the dark side of Dionysos? To answer this in archetypal terms, one must go back once again to ancient Greece and the classic model of healing: Aesklepios.

Aesklepios

Aesklepios, the god of healing, was born the son of Apollo and of a mortal woman, Koronis. Her name could mean both *Dark One* and, in the form of Aigla, *Luminous One.* Apollo himself, although principally known as a solar god, also appeared in a dark form, as a wolf, a chthonic animal. Thus Aesklepios issues from the principles of both light and darkness, celestial and terrestrial.[82]

Raised in a valley under the tutelage of the half-horse, half-god Chiron, he learned there the secrets of nature and gathered energy for his function as bringer of healing forces. As a result of his parentage and upbringing, he is a god of the borderline. Unlike the bright side of his father that manifests in eternal Olympian light, or the darker side of Dionysos as the god of utter darkness in the underworld, the main aspect of Aesklepios comprised the *process* of light coming from darkness. He is god of the "paradox of the mid-zone,"[83] where the two worlds meet as represented by the cold snake that in the Aesklepian cult symbolizes the warm light of life.

To his temple in Epidaurus the sick would flock and under the direction of his priests they would be instructed to withdraw into the "incubatorium." Here the patient was to be alone, "to surrender to a process at work within him,"[84] and in principle the cure was manifested by the appearance of the god in a dream. The striking aspect of Aesklepios, as opposed to his father Apollo, was his empathy with the sufferer. If his father represented stern, detached Olympian authority, Aesklepios was closer to life on earth. As Kerényi says in his description of a statue of Aesklepios:

> The eyes seem to look upwards and into the distance without definite aim. This, combined with the vivid movement, gives us an impression of a great inner emotion, one might almost say of suffering. This god does not stand before us in Olympian calm. He is assailed as it were by the suffering of men which it is his vocation to assuage.[85]

Obviously, one cannot literally equate AA, or any healing method for that matter, with the Epidaurian cult. Besides the enormous cultural differences between ancient Greece and modern Western society, there are obvious differences in method. For example, the candidate for AA does not withdraw alone to an inner sanctum to await a dream. On the contrary, the alcoholic has often been far too withdrawn in the isolation of her illness and it is the group and fellowship, that feeling of belonging to a collective, that begins the healing process.

Still, there is a kind of withdrawal from the conventional collective context, "the madding crowd" that usually proves so difficult for the alcoholic to cope with. AA provides a *temenos,* albeit a collective one, a protected place for the alcoholic, shaky and unsure, to come to and find healing—just as the temple at Epidaurus offered a sanctuary from political or other sources of conflict. AA is also a kind of borderline place, a mid-zone, and many members express this when they say that AA is a "bridge to life." It is not meant to be a retreat or refusal of conventional society. It simply gives support to its members in order that they may live fuller lives in that society, no longer caught between persona emptiness and misfit despair.

Wounded Healers

In the archetypal context it is especially the relationship between Aesklepios and Apollo that creates a link between Epidaurus and AA. Just as the god Apollo may send sickness in his dark, aggressive form, so may he bring recovery and renewal. The experiences of the two women recounted in the previous section illustrate this shift from the negative to the positive aspect of the archetype. The destructive, one-sided solar consciousness that they adhered to in forms of perfectionism and idealization of masculine standards of achievement had provoked a counterreaction, an onslaught of equally one-sided Dionysian influences. But within AA, they found, in a mitigated and more positive form, the other side of Apollo and were able to relate to this in such a way as to remake their lives and find a certain equilibrium again in the collective as well as in themselves.

These positive aspects include the empathy of other members and the actual Program that is the base of AA. The empathy that heals is especially that of the older sober members for the newcomer. They are not sentimental but they are compassionate, and because they have been through the experience, they are able to be, like Aesklepios, "wounded healers" who have experienced the sufferings that it becomes their lot to assuage. By their example they show the newcomer a way between the chaos of Dionysos and the austere, unapproachable perfection of Apollo.

This healing empathy does not involve only a humanizing of the face of Apollo and turning sobriety into a desirable and possible way of life, any more than Aesklepios or his priests became mere "pals" who interceded for Apollo and gathered the sick together for a party of pleasure. The empathy that unites AA members and is passed on from old to new finds its source in something more than just human help. The AA Program bases its work and continuation on what is called simply a Higher Power. Members may interpret this as God, Good, the Group, Luck, the Unconscious or whatever. There is no pressure on members to pledge any specific religious affiliation.

The point is that AA recognizes—as did the priest at Epidaurus—

that some transcendent power must prevail to bring about the cure. This is best expressed in the words of the Second Tradition: "For our group purpose there is but one ultimate authority—a loving God as He may express Himself in our group conscience. Our leaders are but trusted servants, they do not govern."[86]

In the Third Tradition ("The only requirement for AA membership is a desire to stop drinking"), there is a direct link to the Epidaurian-Aesklepian tradition that illness was the only requirement for attendance at the temple and invocation of the god. There were no moral judgments or other discriminating measures—unlike some (by no means all) temples of modern medicine, where certain prejudices of those who treat may be brought to bear upon the sick and prevent them from having access to the healing process. In AA, it is only necessary to *get* there, to bring the body "with an open mind," and then the group and the Higher Power are considered to work their effect—just as the ill person of ancient Greece had to bring himself to the temple and be receptive to the inner process "already at work within him."[87]

The Twelve Steps of AA

For the individual AA member, it is in the Program and Twelve Steps that the spirit is to be found and that Aesklepios-Apollo appear. From the beginning, with Step One—"We admitted we were powerless over alcohol, that our lives had become unmanageable"—and Step Two—"came to believe that a Power greater than ourselves could restore us to sanity"—there is the need to accept an ego deflation.

Then Apollo as arbitrator of higher morality and consciousness speaks through Step Four—"Made a searching and fearless moral inventory of ourselves"—and the following three Steps in which this inventory is shared and the individual seeks to change through the handing-over of his problems and defects to a power greater than his own ego consciousness. This process leads to a kind of acceptance that is necessary before change can take place, and recognition that the ego alone cannot bring about this change. The same process is described by Jung:

> It is tremendously important that people should accept themselves. Otherwise, the will of God cannot be lived. . . .
>
> One is not redeemed by repentance, it must be a change of the system, an acceptance of the things that were unacceptable before. It is not in wiping out the white substance when you accept the black. One does not become enlightened by imagining figures of light but by making the darkness conscious.[88]

This paragraph recalls the description of Aesklepios as the god that flares up out of the darkness, uniting the two realms, denying neither.

The rest of the Steps are concerned with making amends to people harmed by the individual's drinking, maintaining contact with that something greater than oneself, and increasing clarity about his or her own life. Again, there are echoes of this process in the words of Jung:

> We are always trying to be better than we are. We are just as good as we can be and not one inch beyond. . . . That does not mean we cannot improve. . . . Inflations are prejudices about ourselves—our continuous attempts to rise above or below our level.[89]

The Twelve Steps are in effect an attempt to develop some ego humility to counteract the tendencies to grandiosity and inflation that emerge out of the drinking alcoholic's underlying feelings of inferiority and guilt. Although not referring specifically to the alcoholic, Jung gives an apt description of this state:

> He brings in idealism to save himself from the painful sensation of being a lost sheep. Everybody has the tendency to seek good motives for their behavior, instead of saying "I have been a pig." One rationalizes to the God instead of calling things by their right name.[90]

What is needed for recovery, then, is a sense of acceptance of reality and of oneself. The Twelve Steps written by alcoholics for alcoholics recognize this as an on-going process. As it is stated in the AA Program: "We claim progress, not perfection, as our goal." Here Apollo is present in a benevolent form, encouraging endeavor but not driving the individual into self-destructive perfectionism.

The twelfth and last Step is concerned with helping other alcoholics: "Having had a spiritual awakening as a result of these Steps, we tried to carry this message to alcoholics, and to practice these principles in all our affairs." This sounds rather evangelical when taken out of context, but in fact it is the logical continuation in the whole process of being an alcoholic and recovering. Again, Jung could have been speaking of this process when he said:

> It takes a very peculiar kind of experience to make people believe in anything like a spiritual law. It is exactly this experience . . . which would prove the existence of an entirely different type of living, though in itself it is not necessarily spiritual.[91]

This sums up the AA experience—and behind both Jung's words and the AA Steps one can glimpse the Epidaurian experience as well. For the healing there was never merely physical, it was also psychic—a plunge into the unconscious, to which the candidate submitted and from which he returned to the world healed, but also changed, having undergone a process of surrender to powers beyond human understanding.

Feminine versus Masculine Spirit

In some ways, one could also find analogies to the Eleusinian Mysteries. In each case there was a descent into and return from darkness. However, as Kerényi points out, "The way was the same but the sick man who found health at Epidaurus turned back sooner than the Eleusinian initiate who made his way to the Queen of the Underworld."[92]

In other words the experience was less deep, for it concerned "healing" not "wholing." And the difference lay most of all in the gender principle of each. In the Eleusinian Mysteries it was the feminine that presided, the Mystery of Immortality as represented by the ever-renewing cycle of Mother-Kore. At Epidaurus, on the other hand, it was the masculine spirit that prevailed and that flared up in victory *over* darkness. If the sharp Apollonic spirit was attenuated by the "dark warmth" of his more empathetic son Aesklepios, the principle remained that of Apollo, the purpose being to allow for a transformation of this principle.

When I read about this predominance of the positive, masculine spirit at Epidaurus, as opposed to the feminine found in the Eleusinian Mysteries, it was a discovery that illuminated an idea I had long had about AA but could never really formulate. It confirmed my feeling that in fact AA offers an Epidaurian type of healing experience; that is, a masculine, basically Apollonian way of healing by transforming what have become negative, rigid, collective forms into positive ones that foster greater consciousness and aspiration toward a meaningful, spiritual life.

Then the fact that alcoholism was always considered an illness that struck men, and that AA was founded by men and created as, above all, a spiritual program, began to make sense to me. It was not just a cultural fluke determined by role distribution that the alcoholic was always referred to as "he." Beyond the very real prejudice and male chauvinism regarding women, there is an archetypal context for such a persistently masculine dominance in every area of the subject of alcoholism. Until recently, men were more susceptible to an exaggeration of Apollonian ideals. But regardless of sex, it is the masculine way that cures within AA.

Heeding the words of Paracelsus who said, "To find the cause, look at the cure," one may deduce that for a woman (and often for a man as well), *alcoholism is a negative form of identification with the masculine.* AA works and cures precisely because it is a spiritual program, that is, a *positive* aspect of the masculine. As Jung said in his letter to Bill Wilson:

> You see, "alcohol" in Latin is *spiritus* and you use the same word for the highest religious experience as for the most depraving poison. The helpful formula therefore is: *spiritus contra spiritum.*[93]

In a woman, in Jungian terms, the masculine spirit is carried by the animus, a complex which can indeed take the form of the highest religious aspirations or the lowest kind of demonic possession. When she is alcoholic, what others see as her undesirable behavior—unladylike, coarse and hard-boiled—is, in fact, simply an expression of *a drunken animus.* It is he, neglected or misused, who calls attention to himself with such unseemly behavior. But it is also he who finds meaning and leads her to recovery in AA, truly illustrating Jung's formula, *spiritus contra spiritum.*

A more detailed description of this complex now follows, before some specific illustrations of its presence and activity in the lives of alcoholic women.

The Masculine Spirit in Women

The animus, according to Emma Jung in her book *Animus and Anima,* is the complex which in a woman is the opposite pole of the persona, that is, it has the characteristics lacking in her outer and manifest personality. It is composed of the unconscious masculine traits, determined by the latent sexual characteristics, the personal experience of men, plus the collective image of men as it prevails in any given culture.

There are four basic forms in which this masculine image can appear: power, deed, word and meaning. From the football hero to the politician to the orator to the guru—these are the basic archetypal patterns that attract the woman's inner masculine projection. Potentially, the animus contains the germs of wholeness, offering to the woman the possibility of completing herself through development of other, contrasexual capacities. But more often than not, because masculine values are so overvalued at the expense of the feminine in our culture, the animus tends to become tyrannical and overbearing—whether in the form of outside men to whom a woman submits, or an inner voice that constantly devalues her as a woman and rides her with "shoulds" and "oughts" that keep her from having confidence in her own individual way.[94]

Alcoholic women seem particularly to be under the thrall of this perfectionist animus in the form of impossibly high, Apollonian standards. Unlike women who refuse the challenge of the animus and prefer to remain in the passive security of the primal feminine, an alcoholic woman is driven by the animus to accomplish something, whether as a "perfect" wife and mother or a top professional woman. But, as Esther Harding points out, the animus is not a real man, therefore it tends to be exaggerated, "more royalist than the king" so to speak, and an Apollonian animus will be all the more perfectionist and rigid because it is *not* intrinsic to the deepest natural part of woman.[95]

In its positive form, the animus lends a woman the masculine attributes of "knowing what one wants and doing what is necessary to achieve it,"[96] but in its more dubious aspect it can lead a woman away from life and her natural eros or relationship values. Then the masculine standards, which are so idealized that they become unreachable, are compensated for by another opposite and inner animus, aptly described as a "ghostly lover." Like the Pied Piper, he sings his seductive song to attract women into a fantasy world where all is possible but nothing is realized.[97] He isolates the woman in daydream and fantasy, offering an escape from the dullness of a reality where knights on white horses never come and sleeping beauties wait in vain for the prince. In his alcoholic form, this brings us back to Dionysos, one of the most powerful and seductive animus figures, famous for his power over women and for his devotion to them. Unfortunately, this devotion may have devastating consequences on their physical and psychic lives, as it saps the energy they need to deal with the difficulties and problems of everyday life. According to Emma Jung:

> When this happens, the world into which we go is a more or less conscious phantasy or fairy land, where everything is either as we wish it to be or else fitted out in some other way to compensate the outer world. . . . We notice, perhaps, that we have been drawn away somewhere but we do not know where, and even when we return to ourselves we cannot say what took place in the interval.[98]

What better description of an alcoholic blackout! But without even going so far, one recognizes this seductive call to fantasy in the words of women drinkers:

> *A doctor:* "When I was drinking, I was the chief; more than that, I was the most intelligent doctor, the most beautiful woman, the most charming girl, the best daughter, the best friend. . . . "

> *A secretary:* "Full of booze, I thought I was the kind of person I wanted to be. I thought I was charming, I thought I had a lot of friends. I guess I even thought I was half-way beautiful."

> *A minister's wife:* "The first gin and ginger ale at a fraternity party in college convinced me that alcohol was the open sesame to the glamorous sophisticated world of my daydreams. . . . "[99]

The problem consists of transforming this ghostly lover animus into a dynamic force that helps rather than hinders the woman. How this might happen is described by Emma Jung:

> By the blood received, that is, by the psychic energy given to it, the spiritual principle loses its dangerously compulsive and destructive character and receives an independent life, an activity of its own.[100]

This is just what often takes place within Alcoholics Anonymous. From a compulsive dependence on outside men or masculine values there is a shift to a recognition of values that are superior to personal ones. This rescues a woman from seductive ghostly-lover involvements or identification with a man. This, in short, is the religious attitude, a devotion to transcendent values.

That it does bring new meaning and satisfaction is certainly witnessed by the enthusiastic testimonies of women who relate their experiences in AA. In particular, they tell how the *program* and the *men* in AA have been the key points to recovery. Very few mention how other *women* helped. Thus, not only is the spiritual part of the program a base that transforms the destructive, magician-Dionysos animus power, but the real men in AA seem to carry the projections of this as well. Here are some revealing comments by women in AA:

> "Before I was extremely proud of my independence and self-sufficiency, but something that day made it possible for me to ask a man, a friend who was in AA, for help. He answered that cry and did some wonderful Twelfth Step work on me the next week, missing an airplane and canceling other important engagements to get me started on the road to recovery. I got straight Dutch-Uncle, no-nonsense AA talk from him, but also a shoulder to cry on and a strong arm to steer me into the meeting-room for the first time."

> "It didn't matter that I was the only woman among a group of men, in a Latin country where alcoholism among women is ignored or hidden away in psychiatric clinics. The word *padrino* is used in this country to describe the sponsor relationship in AA. The word also means 'godfather' and I found this interpretation perfectly apt. I was as dependent as a newborn babe on my *padrino* and my AA group."

> "I opened the door and there were six men. I listened and listened to what they said. One of the men told me, 'You can do with the bottle whatever you want to do, drink it or pour it out. It's your life—not mine.'"

> "Since coming into the Fellowship, I have been the only woman at most of the meetings in my part of this Western state. When I visit a meeting outside my own group, occasionally it seems that I am expected to reveal some deep dark secret about women alcoholics. This I cannot do because I am not aware of any such secret. But I have never been made to feel out of place or unwelcome because of my sex. And I have never heard anything in a discussion of AA philoso-

phy that I could not apply to myself because I am a woman. The men in my group gave me friendship, loyalty, moral support, confidence and respect when I needed these badly and I am deeply grateful."[101]

When it isn't an actual man or men that are cited as major influences in the transition from drunkenness to sobriety, it may be such things as certain AA slogans, catchy phrases that sum up practical experience and underline the need to hold on to reality:

"I started living when I stopped crying and started trying."

"There are two things I've learned from this Program. First, to surrender completely to the fact that I was fighting a losing battle with the bottle, and through defeat I won. Second, to change myself, because the world isn't going to change to suit 'poor little old me.' I have to put away childish things and grow up."[102]

All of the above remarks recall Jung's definition of the masculine as "knowing what one wants and doing what is necessary to achieve it." The AA Program seems to represent the aspect of the animus related to word and meaning, while the slogans and gestures and the men who say and do them represent a positive version of the animus as power and deed. Thus the four forms are found together. If, as Emma Jung says, "The feminine element can only get into its right place by a detour that includes coming to terms with the masculine factor, the animus,"[103] then the AA context would appear to provide the setting for this, at least in terms of the Dionysian-Apollonian conflict and the split animus that this implies.

The problem that remains, of course, concerns the woman herself. If the healing power of AA, like the Aesklepian cult, derives from pre-eminently masculine values, and if her alcoholism is mainly an animus affliction, what about her femininity? Where has it been and what does it become?

To answer these questions, the last chapter takes a closer look at the stories of some women alcoholics, all members of AA. Their histories are supplemented by dream material taken from cases of other women alcoholics with whom I worked in analysis.

4

The Woman Alcoholic

Four Case Histories

The four women whose stories are presented here all come from basically the same social background—middle and upper-middle class. They all live in Paris, though not all are French. One might object to this as a limited picture of the environment that "makes" an alcoholic, and one could ask about slum dwellers and those at the highest social level, both known to be especially prone to alcoholism. One might also enquire into the effect of particular cultural pressures in different countries.

However, among the many alcoholic women I have known, in whatever country, I have found no substantial variations in style and attitudes toward drinking. This experience and the material I have read on the subject have convinced me that the psychology and the archetypal patterns behind the illness are more or less the same, regardless of outer circumstances. These four women are typical examples; I chose them simply because they were AA members accessible to me and interested in my project. If anything, they are more international than French, and are evidence that AA, like Jungian psychology, has found its way into many cultures because it corresponds to some deeper human realities than those created by national identity or language.

Colette

Colette lives in a large renovated apartment near the Place des Vosges, a part of Paris that was near decay until a few years ago, when affluent couples and professional people began to move in and redo the once-elegant but run-down buildings. Colette's husband is a successful businessman, a German who made his way in the media in Paris where he met and married her. Fortyish, she looks 30, dressed in the latest fashion; she leads a busy life tending to her two teenage children and her husband, entertaining and maintaining a full-time social schedule.

Parents and Childhood

Colette's father comes from a family of opposites. His father was the descendant of an aristocratic family, but his mother came from a very simple working-class family. He himself inherited from both sides. He worked hard all his life, was very "responsible" and industrious, and eventually became the director of an important business. But he kept the "cultivated tastes and 19th-century gentlemanly attitude of his paternal ancestors," according to Colette. These sides remained a cause of conflict that was never resolved but often expressed in his attitudes and behavior. He never really gave himself entirely to his profession. Life at the office, with its petty intrigues and dry administrative details, left him frustrated.

"He should have been a philosopher or a theologian," says Colette, and his disappointment in himself and his life seems to have resulted in an obsessive-compulsive syndrome—perhaps the only way to keep the "forbidden" longings or regrets at bay. With the family he was never outspoken or tyrannical. He was reserved, showing little emotion or affection. "He expected the best from us," praised little and criticized often, but always "gently." His favorite phrases were, "One should be able to . . . ," "If one could . . . ," somehow expressing his own longing for another kind of life and instilling that longing in his children. Says Colette: "I felt so much more scope in him than he actually lived . . . but he never made an effort at actually changing. . . . "

From him Colette inherited her intellectual curiosity and the restless urge to go beyond her limited bourgeois horizon. Father and daughter were never able to communicate on a deep personal level. They were both inhibited by a certain emotional shyness, says Colette, and "the distance had to be respected." Still, she felt much closer to him than to her mother. In fact, she often wondered why her father, so fine and cultivated, married "such a dumb woman." For her mother was very different. In a way, the marriage was similar to that of her father's own parents, in that her mother came from a very simple background. In both training and temperament, she was more practical and down-to-earth. She excelled in doing, not in reflecting, probably (in Jungian terminology) a rather one-sided sensation type. She was not as intelligent as Colette might have wished, "but she was always very *busy,* occupied all the time in the house and garden." In spite of the differences between the parents, however, Colette says "there were never any basic tensions between them. I think that one of the most positive points about my mother is that she never spoke badly about my father."

With Colette, her mother was not very outwardly warm or affectionate. She showed her feelings rather by "giving me nice things or being pleased when I looked pretty." She also insisted that her daughter learn the household skills that she herself was so expert in. At the time Colette revolted, not caring for such domesticity. But today she says she is grateful for this early training. In particular, she thinks that her highly developed, almost professional sense of fashion comes from her mother, who worked as a fashion designer before her marriage. The relationship between mother and daughter was never close, however. Colette resented her mother's busyness and retaliated by flouting her and being "insolent." She found it difficult to have a mother who "never could just *be*. She was always bursting in on me, urging me to *do* something." As a result, Colette says, "I took up the banner for the intellectual and reflective life that she devalued and that my father did not fight for."

The tensions between mother and daughter came to a head years later, during Colette's last drinking years. In one of her episodes, her husband called on her parents for help, but Colette spoke to them on the phone and asked that only her father come. When both parents arrived, having driven up from Bordeaux in the middle of the night, Colette blew up at her mother, accusing her of always meddling, being materialistic, fussy and bossy. From then on her mother never interfered again and, says Colette, "That was the only time I'm glad to have lived my shadow."

Nothing in her parents' lives or relationship to Colette strikes the onlooker as particularly pathological. Given the milieu and the values that each parent inherited, their attitudes, however narrow and stifling, were not unusual. Yet her mother's compulsive busyness and household perfectionism must have resulted from frustration at not finding a more individual outlet for her energy—just as her father's dissatisfaction with only business success reflected his frustrated sensibilities. Each parent, in a way, kept within the official limits of their masculine and feminine roles. But this prevented each of them from living consciously their own contrasexual traits—the animus and anima that seemed particularly strong in both.

For Colette, this meant that she set out in life not only with her own life to live but with quite a bit of the "unlived life" of her parents: the ambition of her mother for prestige and glamour, to be recognized for her talents and flair for creative fashion; and the sensitivity of a father who never followed through on his own introspective questionings. And besides, adds Colette, "Neither one ever lived any crazy young years." She more than made up for these gaps in their lives.

Life Story

Her childhood, Colette says, was happy. She had no particular illnesses or problems. She did very well both at school and outside. Because of her good grades, she was one of the few girls to attend the university preparatory classes at the *lycée,* at a time when such education was still mostly reserved for boys. Popular and sought after, she says she enjoyed very much growing up in the provincial middle-class environment where she fit in and was admired. The only drawback she felt was the narrowness of future possibilities. She longed to see more and go further than her family and peers, to break away from the predictable comfortable life that awaited her if she remained at home. Thus, at age 17, she competed for and won a scholarship to spend a year abroad in England.

She returned home planning to go to a theater school to become an actress. The idea was quickly squelched by her family. Instead, urged by her father, she ended up going to business school where she did well, and afterward landed a job as an executive secretary. Still, the desire to do something more exciting, "to break away," was still present. Therefore, when a boyfriend proposed marriage she accepted. He came from her own background and had a promising career in business. Her parents approved. It seemed the normal thing to do for a young woman of her age. But for Colette, it was above all a way to get away once more—from her family and from her country, because her young husband had a job awaiting him in South Africa. After a large home-town wedding, the young couple immediately left and Colette found herself once more embarking on an adventure.

The marriage did not work. Both partners were inexperienced sexually and had little in common besides. But once Colette was there she decided to get the most out of her surroundings. She threw herself into the round of social life that is to be found in most colonies of Europeans abroad. It made her feel sophisticated and grown-up to be so far from home and to try out things that her background would have forbidden. This was when she started to drink liquor as well.

Drinking Story

Colette started to drink in her late teens. It was part of her environment and social life. Neither parent was much of a drinker but they took wine for granted at meals and festive occasions. From that to drinking regularly in any social gathering seemed a natural step for Colette, as she made the transition from adolescent to young woman. This went on through her early twenties as a young bride. It was so much part of her husband's business and social milieu, and part of her initiation into a more sophisticated way of life than the one she had grown up in. But already, she says, she remembers expressly seeking the "carefreeness and lightness" that the wine gave her. It was not *just* a harmless accessory to being an adult.

While she and her first husband grew apart, Colette threw herself with a vengeance into a kind of "Bohemian, dolce vita" way of life. Alcohol was of course a central part of this. She drank more and more in order to appear like one of the inner circle. Just what "dolce vita and Bohemian" meant, she wasn't exactly sure, but for her the terms expressed everything that was daring, nonconformist and contrary to the principles of her childhood. For the first time, she was often really drunk and she began to get frightened at what was happening to her. After months of this life, she woke up one day with such a hangover of self-disgust that she panicked and decided then and there to quit her job, leave this unhealthy atmosphere and return to her own country.

Back in France, she divorced her husband and found a job. It was a prestigious high-pressure position. Drinking was again a regular part of it all, at business lunches and social evenings. Colette participated as much as anyone but not excessively, for her job interested her too much and her independence was too precious to risk compromising. Alcohol at this period belonged to a professional context. It was not an end in itself and Colette had no trouble keeping her priorities in order.

Problems began, however, when she married her second husband, a young German she had met in the business context. They moved from France to a large German city where he wanted to break into "the big league." Colette worked for a while but was obliged to stop after the birth of her second child. She experienced this as a very great frustration for it threatened her "Bohemian" independent streak. With her new role of mother-housewife, she felt a painful loss of freedom, even a loss of identity. She yearned for an affair, anything to "save" her from this unexpected prison. But even if her puritan upbringing would not have deterred her, her genuine love for her husband did. So she was left with her growing disappointment and frustration.

At the same time, her husband was having difficulties succeeding in the new environment and his professional world. So to add to Colette's own problems, there was now a very real uncertainty about the future and financial insecurity. The anxiety that ensued demanded some kind of alleviation and the most available was alcohol. As they were always in a hard-drinking social milieu, no one noticed when she drank more than was good for her. With time on her hands, at home, she took up gourmet cooking. It was, she says, one of the only ways in which she could still express her creativity. It also provided the possibility of sipping wine alone in the kitchen.

Later, when the couple returned to France, the pattern worsened. This time financial insecurity was no longer a problem. Her husband had established himself successfully and they moved into a pleasant house outside of Paris where he worked. However, the isolation of being just a wife with no mobility (she did not drive) and few outside distractions, was even worse than before, when at least they were in the city and the struggle to survive created its own positive tension. She felt confined and oppressed. She started to drink in the morning. Increasingly, the alcohol provided fantasies and daydreams of another, more exciting life in which she was once more active in a glamorous career. Then something in her reacted, and she sought out work as a translator, work that she could do at home while still fulfilling her duties as a mother and wife. The work succeeded in keeping her away from the first drink until the afternoon. Then, however, wine was the "reward" and she drank on all afternoon. When her husband returned he found her already high and he began to react angrily.

Again she tried to pull herself together, this time by getting a full-time job outside of the home. But again it was in a setting where drinking was not only accepted but considered necessary and chic. Her professional competence earned her a good enough salary to provide care for the children, and she was free to satisfy her ambitions in the outside world. But once she had proved this to herself, she began to drink again. At the office, during lunch hour, in the afternoon from a flask in her purse, and then at home every night, because she "deserved it" after such a hectic day.

Now blackouts became frequent. Terrified at what was happening, she entered analysis, hoping to find the solution to her loss of control. The analysis helped for a while, thanks to a strong transference and the excitement of the new material opening up to her. She quit her job, hoping for a return to "normal."

Soon, however, she was drinking as much and then even more than before. Both husband and analyst were helpless. Her husband, not understanding what was happening, could only get angry or critical. Her analyst tried in vain to get to the source of the problem. She felt betrayed by both of them, she says. Neither understood. The situation finally came to a head when both men were away for a few days. Then she went on a nonstop alcoholic spree—day and night for five days. When her husband returned, he was so horrified that he called her analyst in the middle of the night. The analyst came and could not do much. But the humiliation of that scene, Colette relates, finally brought home to her how serious her situation was. Advised by her analyst, she contacted AA, joined a group and has not drunk since.

Current Situation

Looking back, Colette says that her drinking was, for her, a kind of *participation mystique* with her inner dream world and all the ideals of love and life that had been shattered by reality. When she drank, she could be with the perfect lover, enjoy the fantasies of professional triumph, be, in short, a "goddess." Alcohol was the bridge to a world where anything was possible.

In a social context, particularly with men, it also opened up possibilities of experience that she could not allow herself otherwise. It eliminated the taboos and inhibitions, gave her a feeling of being "reckless." She no longer had to maintain a persona but could dare to say what she thought, to be outspoken and even unpleasant—to say things that "were true, but probably better left unsaid." With men, it allowed her to feel uninhibited and Dionysian.

Today, however, Colette is grateful not to be drinking. Memories of the last phase, when fear and addictive craving had replaced the agreeable effects, keep her from any desire to try again. In particular, she says, she does not at all miss the solitary drinking. That was the most frightening aspect, and now, she says, "the price would be too high." Since going deeper into analysis, she still has access to plenty of fantasy life, but now has more control and understanding of it. To be alone again with alcohol, she feels, would just open doors to too much material from the unconscious and take her too far away from reality. She does miss, however, the Dionysian effects of alcohol, the ones that loosened inhibitions and permitted her to let go, be more irrational, freer to dance, play, enjoy herself in an uncontrolled way. She feels somehow still attached to the kind of "ghostly lover" she dreamed of or "met" when under the influence of alcohol. But she seeks to live these yearnings in other ways, such as active imagination. She has gone very far in painting, for instance, and says it provides a vital outlet for this creativity and inner eros.

At the same time, Colette devotes more and more time to her family and is able to find much more satisfaction and fulfillment for her feelings than before. Sometimes she misses the freedom and independence of being alone, or of having an outside job. But for the moment she wants to find her way within the role of wife and mother. She no longer feels it necessary to express her originality by defying the collective conventions. On the contrary, she finds it a challenge to somehow accept and make the most of her given situation.

It is not easy. She often feels torn between the opposites of freedom-responsibility, marriage-passion. Without drinking, it is more difficult for her to be in the role of hostess for her husband, who is by now a very important figure in the business world. Unlike many husbands, however, he has been supportive of her AA experience, and their relationship today is the product of change and work on both sides.

Solange

Solange and her husband live in St. Germain de Près, the half-intellectual, half-aristocratic section of Paris, famous for its 19th-century salons. Today, in spite of the modernization of the rest of the city, it is an area which has retained its old-world charm. The apartment of Solange, old-fashioned and richly decorated, reflects this, as well as the life-style and background of its inhabitants. In her late thirties, Solange is an attractive woman more at ease in Chanel clothes than jeans. Unlike Colette, she was born and raised in Paris.

Parents and Childhood

Her parents come from similar social and cultural backgrounds. Both were children of the "haute bourgeoisie." But temperamentally they were very different. While Solange's father was content to build on the family business and lead a prosperous, well-rounded life, her mother was devoured by ambition for prestige and power. Their marriage foundered on this. When Solange was nine years old, her mother took a lover, a man who in his business was much more well-known and powerful than her husband. Solange learned about this from the servants. She never dared to refer to it, however, and just remembers being terrified of "what was happening behind the closed door" when her mother received her lover.

Later on, her father also took a mistress, a much younger woman. Of this Solange only remembers how miserable he was when the relationship ended. She doesn't know why it ended and, again, did not dare to ask any questions. What she does recall is "seeing him so unhappy but not understanding why." Despite their evident incompatibility, the parents were never divorced. They continued to maintain the façade of married life until he died. After her father's death, Solange's mother's lover turned into a kind of helpful "uncle" for Solange, but she never told any outsider about his real position in the family.

Her relationship with her father was not a bad one. He was, she says, a warm man, but weak. An earthy person, he worked hard and enjoyed relaxing afterward. He sought out social occasions for the pleasure of the company, not for the prestige. He rarely discouraged or encouraged Solange. She was never really able to talk with him; yet she felt his warmth and felt a positive bond between them.

This was in contrast to her experience with her mother who was quite the opposite. Driven by ambition, she never forgave her husband for not having a university doctorate. The money and position were not enough. She aspired to be "Madame le docteur," and when

he retired from business she arranged for him to return to university
to get the coveted diploma. In his first year, however, he died of a
heart attack. Solange's mother continued to run the family business
until old age stopped her.

Solange has absolutely no positive memories of her mother. She
recalls constantly being told that she was "no good." Her mother
was strict and puritanical, insisting that Solange be a "good girl,"
and often accusing her of sexual looseness with boys. By a tour de
force of repression, she managed to project almost all her shadow
onto her daughter, instilling both guilt and fear about relationships
with men. At the same time, the mother's hypocrisy resulted in
Solange being fascinated with such taboos. As a child, however,
Solange was not aware of such complexities. She simply experienced
her mother as neither warm nor loving in any way. The supreme
value she drummed into Solange was ambition. She insisted that "it
is silly to marry for love," tried to mold her in one direction—that of
landing the right man in order to obtain power and security and
prestige. Simultaneously, through psychosomatic bouts of heart disease (nothing organic was ever detected), she tried to hold on to
Solange, threatening to die if ever she left. Solange's own identity,
her femininity, her individuality, had no place in her mother's scale
of values.

Growing up in the shadow of such jealousy, possessiveness and
criticism, Solange might easily have succumbed to her mother's goal
for her. But instead she managed to rebel and get out. It was only
after she had become independent that she began to succumb, and
then it was to alcohol instead of her mother.

Life Story

Materially, Solange lacked for nothing in her childhood. But emotionally, she was a "poor little rich girl," and she says that her
childhood was an unhappy one. Not only was her mother demanding and disapproving, but because both she and her husband were
occupied so much by the family business, Solange was very much on
her own at home.

At school her work was mediocre. She had no particular interest
in any subject and no special friendships. Due to the ambiguous
situation at home, she felt different from the other children and
rarely invited them to her house.

In adolescence, she began to have more of a social life outside the
home. But no sooner had this begun than her mother packed her off
to a convent boarding school on the grounds that she was too
interested in boys. Solange soon rebelled against this forcible exile.
She hated the school with its strict rules and all-girls' atmosphere

and she was homesick. She called home and told her father that if he did not fetch her she would run away and hitchhike—a shocking proposition for a girl of her age and social background. He refused to yield. After six months of further rebellion, however, Solange was allowed to return home and she finished her studies in a private day-school. She was far behind but managed to get help from a male classmate. Thanks to him, she says, she was able to finish. For the first time she worked very hard, catching up on all the times that she had either been too uninterested or too unhappy to learn. This boy was not from a wealthy family. He was on a scholarship and could therefore ill afford to waste time. He instilled in her a sense of vital necessity that she had never had before. The discovery that she could meet the task gave her new confidence.

Upon finishing, she decided to be independent, to earn her own money, even though she did not have to and could have lived on an allowance from her family.

Secretly, because she knew her mother would not approve, she got her first job by looking in the papers and presenting herself for an interview. She was hired, as an assistant to a traveling business-man. The job did not last because the man's idea of an assistant entailed after-hours' work of a more intimate nature. But Solange now had a taste for independence and went on to work as a model. She thought of herself as "glamorous," she says. The main reward of the work, however, lay in the high salary, which opened the door to freedom and hitherto forbidden pleasures. She still lived at home and her job was not at all her mother's (by now a widow) idea of a proper occupation for a young woman. But Solange went her own way, enjoying life in sophisticated circles and bars, where glamour and alcohol were inseparable.

In time she met her first husband in one of these bars. He was a young doctor, in public service. He was also Catholic. Neither family approved of the marriage, due to the religious difference. Solange's mother, trying to make the best of a bad situation, persuaded her son-in-law to stop work in order to go back to school, and to specialize in order to open up an expensive private practice. What she hadn't achieved with her husband, she was determined to have through her son-in-law. He acceded, and with the pressure and lack of personal satisfaction he began to drink more and more. In two years he was dead of alcoholism.

Drinking Story

Solange drank little until she was about 22. At home, drinking was not part of everyday life. Nor was drinking part of her student life or first years of working. It was only when she began to work as a model and was exposed to a life so unlike her own bourgeois background that, like Colette, she discovered the pleasures of alcohol. She got to know the chic "watering-holes" and soon it became a habit to go there by herself at night. Sometimes she had a date, but more often she preferred to dress up and go out by herself, to drink in elegant, solitary splendor until it was time to go home. When she ceased modeling, however, and had more time and less money on her hands, she became less selective in her choice of bars. From the elegant places frequented by jet-setters, she gradually moved to the popular bars of the lower classes. From champagne to cheap wine, nightly, by herself, but still never at home and never during the day.

In her married life, drinking remained the main pastime, the only difference being that husband and wife drank together instead of alone. They had practically no domestic life. Solange was not interested in being a housekeeper and making a nest. They spent the evenings in bars. When he stopped work to study, most days, too, were spent in bars. Solange recalls that during this period she began to have blackouts and to feel for the first time that the glamour was giving way to feelings of "sadness, desperation and fear." But she was as unaware as her young husband of the fact that they were both by now unable to choose anymore whether or not to drink.

His death left Solange with no drinking partner and no goal in life. It was then that she started drinking all the time. She began in the morning and did not stop until she passed out in the evening. She no longer made any pretense of dressing up and going out to bars to drink in company. She would put on clothes only for the sake of decency and go out and buy liquor which she brought home and drank alone. The alcohol became a substitute for her husband, her dreams, her life. The misery seemed endless and finally culminated in a suicide attempt. It was at the hospital that she learned, through her doctor, about AA.

After joining AA Solange got a job as a nurses' aide. She says it helped her more than anything to keep sober that first year. This, plus the fact that in AA she was supported by two men whom she "adored" and who represented all the possibilities of a new life without alcohol. However, this "honeymoon" period of sobriety ended, ironically, when Solange met and became engaged to her second husband. He was considerably older than she but from a similar background, and somehow she felt she could not admit to him that she belonged to a group of alcoholics. That just did not fit in with what *she* thought his image of her was—a refined, well-bred young woman. She drank with him "normally," the wine and champagne and cocktails, all part of their busy social life and marriage preparations.

She was able to continue this way for eight months, controlling her drinking and maintaining a ladylike front. Her husband was happy. They traveled together and she fulfilled the role of his attractive, sophisticated young wife. But the tension between her unshared secret and the demanding social life became unbearable. She started to drink in secret and to hide her bottles. Her drinking got out of hand in public as well and she would experience personality changes of such aggressiveness that her husband even threatened divorce. It was then that she broke down and told him about AA and her drinking problem. He turned out to be understanding and even attended several meetings, encouraging his wife's involvement and increasing his own understanding.

Current Situation

Solange has now been sober for more than nine years. She sees a psychiatrist from time to time and feels he helps her through crisis periods but mostly she counts on her AA friends and her husband for her emotional needs. They have no children. She says she is "afraid of them" and is glad that her husband has already had a family with a former wife and desires no more children.

Her life is very full, however. She accompanies her husband on business trips all over the world, manages their social life and maintains her AA activities wherever she is. She has in fact become trained in alcohol counseling as well, and far from leading the life of leisure available to her, considering her material circumstances, she has committed herself to more and more responsibilities both at home and abroad in international symposiums. If one mentions this with any admiration, she simply answers, a little embarrassed, "My life started only when I joined AA."

Roberta

Today Roberta lives by herself in Neuilly, a chic suburb of Paris. Her apartment is in a modern building, but she is an interior decorator and has furnished it with a combination of antiques and modern pieces which give it both warmth and individuality. It fits her image —neat, trim, well-groomed, stylishly but classically dressed—an image of the young professional woman who could go from the office to the salon with equal ease and elegance. Although a foreigner in Paris, she speaks fluent French and has become a "Parisienne" in every way.

Parents and Childhood

Roberta was born into a middle-class Protestant family in a predominantly Catholic country, Brazil. She received no special religious

education, however, and the main influence her religious affiliation
had on her was to make her feel like an outsider among her peers.

Both her parents came from "good" families. Her father, son of a
doctor, worked his way up in the furniture business and eventually
became vice-president. Roberta says he was a rather "romantic,
adventurous type." Her mother had no career but was very creative
within the home. Roberta thinks she inherited her mother's artistic
talent and aesthetic sense. The marriage broke up when Roberta was
five. Only after her mother died, many years later, did Roberta learn
the reason for this from a relative. Her mother, it seems, had fallen
in love with another man and taken him as a lover. A scandal
ensued and she was condemned as a "scarlet woman." Her husband
moved out. She was left alone to bring up Roberta and her older
sister and this she did with a vengeance. She ended her love affair
and retired into a kind of self-inflicted penitence. She never went
out with men again until Roberta and her older sister were grown
up.

Roberta's father, meanwhile, regularly "stopped by" for lunch,
arousing very ambivalent attitudes in her about her parents' relationship to each other and the family. Roberta says she has "no
picture of her parents together except fighting." She never knew why
her father came back all the time or even exactly why he had gone
away in the first place. As she was the youngest, she was "protected
and kept in the dark about such things." When she was growing up,
she felt very hostile to her father, seeing him as "unorganized,
disruptive and flighty." She had almost no relationship with him.
Only later, when she went to work in the interior decorating depart-
ment of one of his European companies, did she begin to feel some
connection to him. He comes to see her now in Europe quite often
and she has come to enjoy his visits because, she says, she can now
accept him the way he is.

As a parent, Roberta says that her mother was "liberal, neither
critical nor overambitious" for her children. "She had confidence in
us and said she knew we would behave the way we should." On the
other hand, she wanted to share every part of their lives, particularly
Roberta's. Roberta would dread coming down in the morning to the
breakfast table where her mother was waiting to ask, "Well, how
was it?" and go on to probe her for all the details of an evening
party or a school event. Roberta would resist, but her mother sulked
and so she always ended up telling. Roberta resented this, but felt
helpless to refuse and guilty about anything she kept to herself. She
wished her mother had been less intrusive, more objective and
"strict"; in short, more like a father.

Her mother died ten years ago, and in spite of their closeness,
Roberta says her mother "is still a mystery to me. Somehow I never

got to know her." The symbiosis in which her mother attempted to keep her prevented Roberta from knowing her mother as a distinct person, and thence from achieving a separate awareness that would have permitted her to escape from the suffocating maternal hold.

While Roberta says that her mother always told her she could do or be anything she liked, in fact she smothered her daughter's individuality in overprotectiveness and secrecy about the family reality. At the end of her life, she actually expressed her ambivalent attitude when she confided to Roberta's grandmother that she felt confident about her oldest daughter but "was very afraid" for Roberta's future. The double message she gave was of overt permissiveness and encouragement but of unconscious possessiveness and lack of faith in her daughter's abilities.

Still today, Roberta sometimes feels the effect of this "curse" and is subject to overwhelming feelings of inferiority and incapacity in relationships as well as work. She reproaches herself for these feelings, saying, "But I have had every material chance and privilege, much more than many children." She is slowly gaining her own identity but had to go deeper into her mother's expectation of failure before she could begin to emerge.

Life Story

Until her late teens, Roberta was a "normal" child and adolescent. She did have a stubborn streak, she says, and a quick temper which got her into trouble sometimes with the other children. Already at the age of four, she had attempted to run away from home because she didn't get her own way. When her father took her at her word and simply let her go, she returned contrite and deflated.

In high school, she did well in her studies. She was a pretty teenager who had no trouble making friends of both sexes. She usually had one steady boyfriend during this time but sexual involvement beyond kissing was out of the question for her, as it was for most girls in her culture at that time. She enjoyed these years of being popular and "courted."

When she was 19, Roberta worked for a year as a school teacher. It did not suit her as a vocation, however, and she quit in order to go to Europe, where her father had found her a job in an interior decorating company that had business with his own in Brazil. She hated the work in a large company but came into contact there with another woman with similar interests. Together they set up their own small business for interior decoration and she is still engaged in this. She says that sometimes she wishes she could change, regrets not having more education, or not being simply a housewife and mother, as her sister is. These doubts came to the fore at a time when she was faced with new responsibilities that frightened her. Her partner moved away and Roberta had to do the public relations work, as well as run the shop, by herself. It was not a comfortable prospect for her. She preferred to remain in the background and not have to make decisions. But she did stay on and is now satisfied to have done so and proven to herself that she could manage.

During the first years abroad she met her husband-to-be. There had been a fiancé before, an Italian, but at the last moment, just before the marriage, she backed out, feeling overwhelmed by it all. He was her first lover, but the physical experience had not been positive.

Her husband, on the other hand, came from an upper-class French background, and pleased her because he was "such a gentleman." Unfortunately, he was also even more naive than she about sexuality and married life. Altogether they were married for four years and legally separated for two. With him she lived a protected, comfortable life, but she stopped work. In fact, she says, "I *couldn't* work during those years. I never picked up a design book or pen." The divorce was by mutual consent and they are still friends. After the separation Roberta moved into an apartment on her own and began to work again. Her drinking also became more obvious.

Drinking Story

There was little drinking in the home while Roberta was growing up. She remembers only having champagne as a teenager at Christmas and feeling "very happy" on it. It was when she left home at 21 and went to Europe that she discovered wine. She quickly found that this common "harmless beverage—not vulgar like whiskey or beer," made her feel more relaxed.

Soon she was having half a bottle every evening with meals alone. It helped her feel less homesick. At parties it gave her confidence, made her more talkative and animated. People seemed to like her more when she was a little high. She wasn't so introverted and quiet then, and she suddenly knew what to say and lost her insecurity about being a foreigner.

By the time Roberta married she was drinking daily. She drank in the kitchen from her secret bottle of cooking sherry, she drank in company and drank too much at parties, where she still felt awkward and like an outsider. Mostly the wine "loosened her up"; she rarely got loud or outrageous, but most days she was a little tipsy from sipping wine all afternoon. She had had insomnia since getting married, so she would finish a bottle of wine every night just to be able to fall asleep. Her husband, gentleman that he was, did not criticize her. But she was rarely an offensive drunk. Most often she was simply anesthetized and less anxious. She could give parties without being paralyzed if it wasn't "perfect." She could converse without feeling like a fool. Blackouts began, but she managed to avoid any catastrophes since she did not drive a car or create problems for other people.

After the couple grew apart and agreed to separate, her drinking became more serious. She found herself going to parties and getting very high and "talking too much and repeating myself because I was afraid of not being heard." Or she would refuse all social life and drink alone at home. As she was working she did not drink during the day and this meant, for her, that "I didn't really have a problem." But every night she had a date with her bottle. It made her feel relaxed but nostalgic and lonely and she would suddenly think of old and distant friends to call. The need to make contact became imperative. Huge telephone bills were the only evidence of these conversations, since she seldom remembered them. In the morning she would wake up with bruises from falling on the floor and into the furniture. She missed days at work, and finally friends intervened.

Roberta returned to Brazil and her family tried to put her in a clinic. But she wanted one more chance, so she went back to Europe and there an old friend from childhood, coincidentally in Paris and in AA, contacted her. She began to attend meetings and stopped drinking.

Current Situation

Today, Roberta is content with her life though all is not perfect. Most of her satisfaction comes from her job and her apartment. In both these areas, she has made major changes. At work she has taken on increasing responsibilities, which she says she never could have met before she stopped drinking. She has taken on the task of supervising the entire decoration and finishing of her new, larger apartment. Both jobs exhaust her but give her a sense of confidence. In her personal life, she has close friends, particularly from AA. She feels much less isolated but she is anxious and discontented about her "inability to be more open" with people, "to give more." What she experienced as the "loosening" effect of wine is difficult to achieve sober. With men too, she is still unsure and anxious.

She has a boyfriend but he lives far away and has his own psychological problems. Sometimes, she says, she would like to "save" him, to help him out of his emotional paralysis. She seems still to carry some guilt for her mother's failure as a wife and compensates for this by trying to be prince to the man's Sleeping Beauty (his anima). This active role, however, tends to attract men with a passive or undifferentiated sexuality—which in effect "protects" Roberta from the penetration she fears, and which indeed ruined her mother's life.

Yet she misses being treated more "like a woman," with consideration and feeling. She misses being courted, the way she was as a teenager—before her initial, disappointing sexual experience and before marriage, neither of which she was prepared for.

Roberta is at one and the same time both very fragile and feminine, and very tough. Her vulnerability and determination have always been in conflict. Today they are a little closer. She dares more to live out her impulses and to make demands of life. She says, like Solange, that she is above all grateful to AA for giving her a new way of life. Yet one senses that her sobriety and the support she receives from AA, although vital, cannot fulfill some deeper need for an inner reconciliation of opposites.

Noelle

Noelle lives in a large house outside of Paris with her husband, who commutes to the city in his Mercedes. She has her own small car, which she drives proudly and often since getting her driver's license three years ago. She says it represents her freedom from the house and suburbs after years of feeling confined in a "golden cage." She looks much younger than her 55 years. Outwardly, with her expensive "country casual" tweeds, she looks like a typical, wealthy, well-preserved suburban matron. One would expect her to be more involved in the country club than with a group of alcoholics. Her story belies this superficial impression.

Parents and Childhood

Noelle's parents not only come from different social backgrounds but from different countries as well. Her father, son of an Australian self-made man, fulfilled his family's ambitions for prestige by becoming a medical doctor. Her mother came from an old but modest peasant family in eastern France. They met when they were working in the same hospital in Sydney.

Noelle remembers little about her father or his relationship to her. Most of what she knows or remembers comes from her mother. She knows, for example, that she was dressed like a boy until she was three years old, because her father wanted a son, but that, in spite of this, he loved her "very much"—until the birth of her younger sister. From then on, said Noelle's mother, "You were nothing."

Noelle's father was apparently very successful both socially and professionally. People sought after his company and his skills, but at home he was tyrannical and demanding. He wanted a large family, so much so that he refused to let his wife have a Caesarean for her first child, even though the doctor recommended it and his wife suffered 36 hours of labor. He also refused to give her any money to buy gifts for her family back in Europe. But he himself was a "bon vivant." He drank well and enjoyed festive dinners.

In fact, his early death seems to have come about through this kind of indulgence. After a large meal he was suddenly stricken with stomach pains and he died the next day after an emergency operation. Whether it was a burst appendix or something else, Noelle does not know. Her mother maintained an air of mystery about the exact circumstances of his death. She would only say that, as he died, he said to her, "You'll never know how much I loved you."

These words, real or invented, might have been her mother's only reward in an otherwise disappointing marriage. But Noelle is not really sure about this either. Their relationship remains as mysterious and cloudy as her father's death. On the one hand, he was presented (by her mother) as very much the patriarch, who treated his wife as a breeder and housekeeper. There was also some indication, some hints dropped, that he took a mistress after Noelle was born. As for her parents' physical relationship, Noelle was told as a young girl that sexuality was a "nasty, smelly business." Yet her younger sister was told that her parents' sex life was ideal. It seems that the mother's own femininity was so fragmented that she unconsciously expressed opposite aspects with each girl.

In later years, as Noelle grew up, her father was described more and more as a hero who could do no wrong. Because her mother insisted so much on this ideal image, Noelle feels sure "there must have been something else." But it was forbidden to inquire into or to challenge her mother's version. Her picture of her father, therefore, was one of fragments, contradictions and mystery, all interpreted and dealt out by her mother.

Noelle's own relationship with and image of her mother were not so mysterious. They were clearly and simply negative. Her birth was Noelle's first mistake, as far as her mother was concerned. Not only did she cause hours of painful labor, but she put an end to her mother's professional activity. It was also then that her father probably took a mistress in the person of a young and pretty secretary. If Noelle had only been a boy, at least her mother could have benefited from her husband's satisfaction and had a male child to compensate for the husband she received so little tenderness from. She lost no time in venting her hostility and deception on this first-born daughter.

From early on, Noelle was told she was "born dead," and made to listen to the martyrdom her mother suffered to bring her into the world. She was disciplined very severely. Once as a child of four, when she was playing with a little boy, they both began to undress. Noelle's mother came in and beat her and locked her in a room for three days. Noelle says she never got over the shame and humiliation. Her mother added to her misery by saying, "Wait till your father knows," implying even worse punishment to come. Noelle does not remember him ever actually being involved in this incident, or in any other disciplinary action. Her mother simply mentioned her father's potential wrath as reinforcement. Thus Noelle's image of him was that of an all-powerful male deity who had the authority but delegated the power to the woman.

All in all, Noelle's experience was of a very unhappy childhood. After the death of her father, her mother managed to make the life insurance last for several years but this entailed such thrift that Noelle rarely knew the pleasure of a new dress or even a doll. As the oldest of three girls, she was the one responsible for the heaviest chores in and out of the house. Her mother remained at home and devised ways to save money. She also stayed home, however, because she felt a foreigner in her husband's land. So she sewed, she cooked, she made things out of nothing. She was very creative, says Noelle, but even in this she was parsimonious and never passed on her skills to her daughters. When she cooked, for example, no one was allowed in the kitchen to watch her. Noelle was expected to do the dishes. She became a kind of Cinderella scapegoat for her mother's contempt for her own sex.

As a result, Noelle grew up knowing how to work. She worked to avoid reproaches at home, she worked to gain praise and acceptance at school. She also worked after school to earn pocket-money and some appreciation for her efforts—not from her mother, who appreciated nothing she did, but from her employers. There was little time for play and playmates. "Besides," says Noelle, "who liked a goodie-goodie and teacher's pet?" So she had few friends. One exception was a little girl, "whose mother was lovely. She must have weighed 350 pounds and she was always laughing." This was the one positive maternal figure in Noelle's life—the opposite from her own mother, whose control and calculations would never have permitted such emotional or corporeal expansiveness.

Regarding her own personality, Noelle describes herself as "very spunky and fresh" when young. She was an active, adventurous, gregarious little girl. But her mother took her "spunkiness" for insolence and more than once punished her for it. When Noelle was a little older, her mother would push her to recite and perform in front of guests but scold her afterwards for "overdoing" and "show-ing off." Little by little, the ebullient, provocative sides of her nature were beaten or bullied out of her. By the time she was ten, she had already retreated behind the passive, docile, good-girl façade that brought on the least trouble. She says she suffered from being trapped in this persona (which was to dominate a good part of her life) but her fear of being punished for being unacceptably lively, for being in fact herself, was the overriding factor. Even now, her ideal of feminine perfection is "a cool, flawless, sophisticated aristocrat—someone like Grace Kelly. Women like that can do what they want." She herself always feels too "fleshy," not quite right in her clothes, awkward in crowds, "inarticulate or chattering on about nothing. I never know what I'll do next."

Today, it is surprising to hear Noelle talk about herself so dispar-agingly because she does not look that way at all. On the contrary. But, as a child, not only did she feel that way but, she says, "I did everything to make myself unattractive." In high school she had acne, was plump and poorly dressed. She worked twice as hard to compensate but this did not change her feelings of being different from the "popular deb girls." She went out only at night, if possible, so no one could see her.

Not until she was 18 did Noelle escape her Cinderella life. Her Prince Charming was a high-school classmate and hero—"like a Greek god, with blond golden hair and blue eyes. He was adored by all the deb girls." But he chose her. They married, he continued at school and Noelle earned the money, working for her husband as she had worked for her mother. Their relationship was practically nonexistent. They had nothing in common. Neither knew anything of sex, which for her was a shock. She had never had any physical contact with boys, had found them almost repulsive except in "ro-mantic" relationships. Both she and her husband were virgins when they married and not much more experienced three years later when they divorced. They came to agree that it was a youthful mistake and parted amicably.

Shortly after, Noelle met another man, a French friend of her mother's family, who charmed her with his many languages and apparent sophistication. They married, she became pregnant and he left for a new job in another country. Meanwhile, she went back to work to support herself and her baby. When she joined him later, he had taken up with another woman. They were divorced a year later. Noelle would rather have stayed with her husband, "because I wanted to give my daughter a father so that she wouldn't have my experience." But in spite of her efforts to make herself "useful if not loved," the time came when the humiliation was too much and she left.

She went to France and found work as a model. "It was," she says, "the happiest time of my life. It was like coming out of a cage. I could change and look like someone else all day long. I could be seen and not see the people as I walked down the ramp. My employer said I was one of the best, for I could transform my walk and style with each outfit." She finally had a chance to break out of the dull, "good-girl" image that had pursued her all her life. Now she was independent and accountable to no one but herself. This lasted about four years. Then she met and married another man. He was wealthy, which suited her mother's ambitions for her, and also timid, which made her feel less anxious than most men did. After they married they moved into a large, luxurious home in the suburbs of Paris, where Noelle had no more worries about material problems.

For a while Noelle was content to enjoy the comfort and the new role of mistress of her own domain. She threw herself into gourmet cooking, decorating and hostessing, aided by the constant advice of both mother and mother-in-law. But her husband was busy and not given to much social entertainment. Her efforts were largely in vain, and little by little she turned to alcohol to banish her feelings of inadequacy.

Drinking Story

Drinking had never been part of Noelle's life, not as a teenager nor as working woman and two-time wife. As an adolescent her only recourse against maternal demands had been flights into ugly moods and bouts of unaccountable drowsiness. Doctors put these down to growing pains.

As a wife for the third time, with her own internal negative mother driving her on to meet impossible standards (not to speak of the two all-too-real ones outside), Noelle launched into the role of perfect housekeeper, avidly studying homemaking and trying to learn the social protocol that belonged to her new surroundings. But no one really cared. She felt useless and isolated. Then she discovered wine. Just a little at first, but in her new social surroundings it was part of "gracious living," and Noelle was determined to live up to her new environment by getting to appreciate "the finer things." She often felt anxious and unsure, but wine was a friend that did not judge her.

It began when she would finish off the wine served at meals. The family—by now including two children—would scatter after lunch to their various activities, leaving her alone. She would sip the wine and look out the window and daydream. And then, drowsy from the wine, she would sleep a few hours. Then she would have to do the chores, the washing, ironing, cleaning—and would drink a little for "energy to get me going." Then it was time to think about dinner and she would have an aperitif "to inspire me about what to cook." Inspiration, anesthesia, stimulation, tranquillizer; the wine became her friend for all moods, company for daydreams and an ally in discontent. Noelle did not hide her bottles. It was not necessary, since she was alone so much and presided in the kitchen where she always had a drink at hand.

In time, her husband began to suspect something. Her moods, in the evening especially, were so unpredictable. She would often pick a fight, complain about her in-laws or her husband's neglect of her. Noelle, formerly such a model of docility and wifely obedience, after a day's tippling would turn into a "vulgar virago," according to her husband. He would react with the "silent treatment" the next day, which would put her into such a state of anxiety and guilt that she would drink to cope with that. Since her vulgar shadow was so unacceptable, she resorted more and more to deceit and dissimulation. After a while, she was mildly drunk almost daily from noon on. Periodically she would fly into a rage and break dishes in front of her horrified spouse. This went on for twenty years.

Noelle describes herself during that time as "a benumbed housewife, sleeping away the time"—drinking to face life, drinking to flee from it. Then her mother died and for a year she was in a state of shock. Although she had hated and resented her mother, now she found herself alone and lost without the old lady's constant meddling.

One day, in the midst of a depressive, alcohol-befogged mood, the idea of AA "just popped into my head out of nowhere. I went to the phone and called and asked what I had to do to join the club?" The man on the other end replied "Nothing." He asked her to tea and introduced her to the program. A little older, dumpy-looking but kind and patient, she says he was exactly the kind of person she needed. "If he had been good-looking, I would have fled." She told him about her life and he said she was probably an alcoholic. At that she answered, "At last, I'm *something.*"

From then on Noelle attended meetings and for the first time in her life felt "at home." Her husband, much to her surprise, reacted very favorably and encouraged her to continue.

Current Situation

Today Noelle has her own life, devoting much of her time to AA and church activities. Both are places where she feels she can "serve."

In the more intimate areas of her life, however, she is less satisfied. Her marriage is better since she stopped drinking, but basically it is better because she has accepted its limitations, not because husband and wife have "rediscovered" each other. She says that she wanted an "ally" in her husband and never found one. Although he is a good provider and a pleasant social companion, his energy goes more into work and his passion for reading and erudition than into his marriage. Noelle used to complain about this, she hated the books as rivals for his attention. Now she accepts the situation and leads her own life. Her children are grown up and gone from the house and she does not regret their leaving. They each have had, and still have, some emotional problems, but she no longer blames herself for everything that goes wrong in their lives—a guilt she gladly shouldered while drinking.

But something in Noelle is still dissatisfied, still searching. "I feel like a spook," she says. "I'm not here. Nothing has happened in my life. I'm always waiting for something to happen. I was asleep for so many years. Now that I'm awake and sober, I'm always waiting for a great event. I sometimes don't even feel married." This is what she says, in spite of her full life, including three marriages.

*

Now we come to a dilemma that in my experience is common, but often unexpressed, among women in Alcoholics Anonymous. Their drinking is arrested. Their need to belong to something, to feel unconditionally accepted, to participate in a community that has both emotional and spiritual meaning—these needs have been met. Once lonely Cinderellas or Sleeping Beauties, each has found a safe refuge where she is appreciated and recognized.

And yet something is still missing. Apparently even AA is not quite enough. What or who is it in the woman that exists alongside the alcoholic that remains to be satisfied?

Psychological Factors

Although the four women whose stories have been presented here in detail have a common background, they are individual and different personalities. Each one could be studied as a unique case. My purpose in interviewing them, however, was more to find out what they had in common, besides their social class, than how they differed.

The same general factors concerning traditional roles of men and women, and the changes that are painfully coming about in these roles, apply to the lives of these four women. But more specifically, I looked for clues within shared attitudes, family structure, childhood experiences and events in their lives which might have contributed to their drinking.

In other words, if in any illness there is a "predisposition" waiting to be provoked by outside circumstances, what common psychological factors predisposed these women to alcoholism?

The Mother Complex

The mother is not only the source of life but, for a woman, the source of her sexual identity. It has already been pointed out by many authors that alcoholics are likely to have been deprived of maternal nurturing, either literally or figuratively. Certainly these four women are no exception. In each case, there is a very strong negative mother complex.

Even Roberta, the only one who did not experience her mother as cold and hostile, is adamant about not wanting to be like her. If the mothers of the other three were animus-ridden and projected their own feelings of feminine inferiority onto their daughters in an outwardly critical manner, Roberta's mother did the same in a more subtle way. It was nonetheless felt by her daughter and confirmed by Roberta's lack of confidence in herself as a woman.

In addition, none of the mothers were really fulfilled in their lives either as women or as human beings. Their husbands disappointed them on the one hand, and on the other they had no positive outlets for their unusually strong animus energies. Their daughters bore the brunt of this frustration. Not only were they less loved as girls, but they were instilled with a fear of men, or contempt for them, that influenced their own relationships as grown women.

All four women left home at an early age, a more or less conscious move to escape the destructive maternal influence. Unfortunately, leaving home does not undo its effects for mother and daughter are two archetypal forms of the same basic constellation. If the two poles are necessarily separated by the daughter's initiation into womanhood, usually through the intervention of a man, still they are destined to be rejoined—as depicted in the yearly return from Hades of Kore-Persephone to her mother Demeter. The mother-daughter archetype represents the feminine mystery that is the ebb and flow of life itself, its dying and renewal.[104] For the archetype to be split, for the daughter to be cut off entirely from her mother—an older side of herself—amounts to a wound in the primal feminine. Thus a woman who seeks, because of a negative personal mother, to escape from the maternal sphere, may literally save her life but she pays the price of hurting something within her own deepest being.

The following two dreams give graphic images of the negative mother complex so frequently found among alcoholic women. The first belongs to a woman age 35, an active alcoholic when she began analysis:

> I was in a butcher's shop. My mother was ordering some meat. I wanted to but couldn't. I looked around and saw my dog and another one just like him lying on the floor. The side of each animal was bloody as if devoured. I shuddered and turned away.

The butcher's shop is a place where the "flesh," the raw meat, is made available to the customer in cookable, edible form—where the *prima materia,* the building blocks of matter and body, is prepared for individual use. But the final result, the steak and chops, come from a killing of animals, a death on one level that makes life on another possible. Unfortunately, access to this transformative process is barred by the dreamer's mother—literally her parent but psychologically her own mother complex. The mother figure's rapport with the butcher keeps her daughter in the background, unconscious and innocent, a spectator to the transaction which involves sacrifice but also promises a continuation of life. From a mythical point of view, one could say that mother-Demeter keeps daughter-Kore from contact with the raw stuff of life.

Unable, then, to go beyond her negative mother complex and receive the transformed animal flesh, the dreamer is faced with a more frightening and negative image of the instincts: her dog, representing feeling and instinctive levels, is ravaged and murdered, but without any ultimate "goal." It seems that her mother complex had so alienated her from her body and the natural process of decay and renewal, that her instinctive life was in danger of being eaten up and even destroyed.

In fact, this woman had lived in such a fantasy world, such a flight into chemical spirit, that her body had indeed been severely neglected and abused. It was clear that if she continued to live in this way an untimely death was a real probability. The "doubling" of the dog image indicates that the unconscious wants to bring this urgent message home without delay or subtleties. The question for this woman was, did she *want* to live? Or *want* to heed the "matter"? In the dream the prognosis appeared ambivalent. She *saw* the raw, mortified flesh but turned away. At the time I was optimistic, since she had decided to undertake analysis. But after six months she was obliged to return to her home country, across the ocean. There she began not only to drink more but to take heroin as well. The result of her double addiction was suicide within a year from the time of the dream. The negative mother had won.

The second dream belonged to a woman who came into analysis six months after joining AA:

> I'm in a cabin in the woods with a man. He is tall and very handsome. I think it is Alexander the Great. A horrible witch bursts in. Blood drips from her mouth and her teeth are like fangs. She lifts a bloody knife to murder the man. I run from the cabin screaming, "Help, she's killing Alexander." On the edge of the forest outside, a woman stands and waits for me. She is smiling. She is dressed in a long white robe and looks like a fairy godmother. I run toward her.

This dream certainly depicts a negative mother in her most classic witchlike form. But in spite of her horrible aspect, she turns out to have a certain positive function.

The dreamer is in a cabin in the woods, a kind of nature paradise, alone with the hero, Alexander the Great. The situation is an Eden of complicity in which the woman's positive masculine energies are all projected onto an idealized, perfect kind of man. If she stays there, the dreamer risks never living her own life, never escaping from the fascination of a fairytale ghostly lover. Thus the witch mother forces the dreamer out into the world and simultaneously slays this heroic Alexander—a classic example of the *felix culpa* or "fortunate crime" motif. If it means a loss of certain inflationary animus ideals, it may also be the beginning of a relationship with a more positive mother in herself, one through whom the dreamer can realize her essential femininity in cooperation with a more realistic and helpful animus.

In fact, this actually did happen over a period of four years in analysis. Gradually the femininity which had been so wounded in her childhood began to heal, and as it did the need for such an extraordinary animus companion lessened, allowing her some satisfaction in her work and in her relationships with men, both of which had been very problematical. Indeed, the personification of her animus as Alexander the Great, a true solar hero, itself points to the dreamer's heroic potential, which she actualized by staying sober and persevering with her analysis. It is again an example of the Apollonian element that may push a woman into alcoholism when she becomes *too* Olympian and heroic, but that also enables her to come out of it by relating to positive aspects of the masculine spirit.

Finally, let us look at two dreams of a 42-year-old woman who entered analysis six years after joining AA. Since sobriety she had been an ardent and committed member, helping countless other alcoholics actively and as an example. But when she came to me she felt empty inside and depressed. She said she no longer knew herself, she had lost her famous verve and unbeatable "masculine" determination. In many ways, she was entering a classic transition from first to second half of life; in her case this was marked by a change from animus identification to a development of the feminine. At the beginning of analysis she brought the following dream:

> I'm on top of a mountain in deep snow. I'm hungry and cold. I look for a restaurant but all the public ones are closed. I see a light in a chalet and go in. There, an old woman sits at the head of a table where everyone is eating. I join them. It's warm and cosy.

Here we see the dreamer isolated in a high, cold place. The elevated Apollonian spiritual values that she strove so hard for (as a faithful AA member, in particular) are hostile to the feminine ego.

And the feelings, basic and biological, "hungry and cold," lead her to seek refuge from such an atmosphere. The public restaurants are closed; that is, the collective antidote to her plight is no longer a possible solution. But light—here a warm light, more Aesklepian than Apollonian—comes from a private place, an intimate, more feminine retreat, where an old woman presides. The dreamer joins the people and is nourished by her own archetypal positive mother. For a woman who reveled in racing down high mountains on skis and dared all sorts of adventures "like a man," this dream portended an important shift.

Many months later, shortly before leaving analysis, she dreamed:

> My mother is nude, standing on the beach. I go up to her. She hugs me. I hug her and we both laugh.

This dream made me feel quite positive about the continuing evolution of her long-neglected feminine being. Here the scene is more human. The beach is a place between water and earth, the border between the unconscious and consciousness. It is far more amenable to life than a high, cold mountain top. In outer reality it was also a place she loved to go, to walk and simply be by herself. So it has a special sense of introversion as well. That here the woman is actually her own mother and not an unknown archetypal image is also confirming her ability to accept and humanize the maternal within herself. Since she had always experienced quite a lot of difficulty in giving her love and patience to her own daughters, while favoring and pampering her son, this was a much-needed reconciliation for both outside and inside life. She later wrote from her home country that she was able to foster a much better relationship with these two young daughters, having realized how much of her own feminine "inferiority" she had projected onto them.

This is one of the more striking illustrations of a woman alcoholic, wounded in her femininity by a negative mother, "redeeming" this mother and finding a sense of inner wholeness that AA alone could not give. I would not pretend that most women come to this point. On the contrary, many, like Noelle, remain stuck—not on a beach, where the elements join, but in a "no-woman's-land" where they remain sober and active in AA but are still always looking for the elusive "something" that would give them a greater sense of themselves as women, not only as sober human beings. But the example above shows what *can* happen when the problem of the negative mother complex is worked on consciously.

Regardless, however, the animus—both its negative and positive sides—remains a vital part of the alcoholic woman's psychology and it has its source in the father complex. Let us now look at how this manifests in the lives of Noelle, Solange, Colette and Roberta.

The Father Complex

In each case, the father, in contrast to the mother, is perceived as positive. Even in Roberta's story, which differs a little from the others, her father emerges as the more positive of the parents. While under her mother's influence she resisted him, but this changed soon after she left home and they have become closer with the years.

For all of them, it is as if the child was so wounded by a bad experience with the mother that she had to project all her positive expectations onto the father. As adults, they remembered their fathers either as rather weak men, or as mysterious, but as little girls they perceived his weakness or mystery as lovable, somehow caused by the mother and not his fault. Any feelings of warmth and affection came from the paternal, not maternal, side. In Noelle's case, because of her father's death and her traumatic relationship with her mother, she had only the nostalgia for a father whom she never really knew, to give her some much-needed parental warmth. As in the other cases, however, the father was not very communicative with his daughter, and furthermore not perceived as successful in terms of the wife's ambitions. The daughter, to protect her one positive image, *had* to idealize him; internalized, this ideal actually became more influential than the real man. It is an example of an archetype taking over when it is not mediated by the human being.

An example of the inflated and idealized father image appears in an initial dream of an alcoholic analysand who did *not* join AA:

> I'm at home, about to leave for a voyage. Santa Claus appears. He is very tall, like a skyscraper, almost too tall for me to see his face. He beckons to me and I follow, eager for the adventure. First we cross through my home town, then he heads off to the mountains. It's hard to keep up with him. We arrive at a plateau. The wind is blowing so hard I am almost blown down. I say "wait, wait," but he walks on without looking back.
>
> Finally he stops in front of a cave in a mountain side. He says a magic word and it opens. But when I get inside he has disappeared. I look all over. The cave is like a toy shop with little wooden toys on shelves. A woman appears. She is dressed like a salesgirl in a folklore costume. She is middle-aged and plain-looking. She makes a sign for me to come near and then she puts her head to the wall. I do the same and I hear some cries. I think it is women crying for help. I wake up in a fright.

In this dream the dominant figure is the Santa Claus, the "good father" who brings presents to children if they are good but disciplines them if they are not. As he is larger than life-size in the dream, so the father image is more than human for the dreamer.

What is more, it is very much a collective image, one valid for all children. Hence the personal father complex is identified with a collective archetype, one that leads the ego away from home, civilization, to the windy plateau. This recalls Emma Jung's remarks about Wotan, the Nordic god of the wind who represents *pneuma* (spirit), which can be a destructive force that overwhelms the woman and leads her on a kind of spiritual wild goose chase, as in this dream.[105]

The man leads her to a cave, potentially a more maternal refuge and shelter from this powerful and elemental spiritual force. But here it turns out to be a toy shop, a place of fantasy where reality, so to speak, is "belittled." The only person in the shop is a woman, a rather ordinary one in a silly costume, yet she does indicate to the dreamer the presence, deep in the unconscious, of a suffering feminine element—the heard but unseen voices of the women crying. Thus the existence of the collective and inflated masculine seems to go hand-in-hand with a trivialized feminine consciousness, concerned with a childish world.

At the same time, however, in leading her away from home and primal safety, the Santa Claus figure does show her what the problem is; although he might be the "cause" of the inferior feminine, he also leads the dreamer closer to discovering the source of her pain. As the four women's stories illustrate, they were all caught between their animus aspirations to be perfect in whatever they undertook, and the rigid persona and cramped kind of feminine roles they chose to fulfill their aspirations. The dream depicts this situation, but it also points to the possibility of escaping the persona image of a "salesgirl"—a woman at the service of others who must sacrifice her own individuality in order to please both customers and employer—by exploring and heeding the hidden, and perhaps less conventional, aspects of the feminine.

Like Alexander the Great, the Santa Claus figure incarnates a very idealized masculine image. One heroic, the other paternal, they are dominant factors in the psyches of alcoholic women. Thus when a woman does join AA, she is content to relate to the men, to heed their advice and to even resist the idea that AA, as basically a man's organization, might have some drawbacks for women. Alcoholic women are fathers' daughters. They sometimes identify with men. As Colette says, "You feel resentment about being a woman and your field of endeavor being so limited, while a husband can go out and conquer the world." But they idealize them as well. All four women interviewed agreed that in their first marriages they were looking for the Prince Charming of their dreams, who would make up for the fathers and be exciting, caring partners as well. With such

high ideals it is not surprising that none of these marriages worked
out. In fact, they all married men, at least their first husbands, who
were bound to disappoint them through their lack of developed
masculinity. Thus each repeated her mother's pattern, caught in an
unconscious identification with her while trying so hard to be different.

Parental Marriage

The marriage of each woman's parents, seen through the eyes of the
child, was unsatisfactory. Not only was the relationship between
parents and child negative or unrealistic, but so was the parents'
relationship to each other. In the case of Roberta, this lack of
understanding and communication was obvious. In Noelle's story
the fact that her father died when she was so young makes it
difficult to assess, but from the warnings her mother gave her about
men, plus the contradictory versions of perfect happiness and total
unhappiness, it seems doubtful that her parents were happy with
each other. Colette's parents, on the other hand, maintained the
image of a satisfactory marriage, both to themselves and to the
outside world. Yet Colette's feeling that her father married beneath
his intelligence, and her mother's meddling and busyness, hint at the
lack of real fulfillment in the relationship.

The point here is that however the parents themselves experienced their marriage, each daughter had a perception of her parents
as being in some way or another unhappy as a couple, and thus
lacked the basic security of a safe "home base" from which to
extract a sense of her own values and feminine identity. Furthermore, and this seems to me especially important, in no case were the
parents actually divorced. They all coped stoically with their marital
difficulties. Solange's parents both took outside lovers. Noelle thinks
her father did, Roberta knew her father did and learned only much
later that her mother did as well. Colette's parents simply let themselves be contained within the institution of marriage, whatever the
individual consequences.

In all the marriages there was something wrong, but it was hidden
away or disavowed, and it was resolved through means that destroyed whatever chance the parents might have had to become a
more conscious couple, less dependent on projections and collective
tradition. In each case, the daughter perceived this "lie," as well as
the subterfuges involved to adjust to it, but was kept from going too
deeply into her own perception of the problem. She shied away from
it, as in the case of Solange, who was afraid of "what was going on
behind the closed door," or Roberta, who never knew why her

father came for lunch but didn't live at home. In short, the truth was simply not available, hidden or repressed in order for the parents to maintain appearances and "protect" the children.

Since a child cannot risk the displeasure of her parents without some danger of being rejected by them, and even, in the mind of the child, losing their love entirely, the daughter who perceives such a major parental problem cannot risk bringing it up. She is forced to deny her own feelings and perceptions in order to remain under parental protection. She is obliged, in a way, to remain unconscious, even as her young ego struggles to detach itself from the *participation mystique* with the family. The price of peace and protection is to stay quiet about the family secret, to be an accomplice to the lie she knows exists but cannot expose.

The Secret

In "Problems of Modern Psychotherapy," Jung speaks of the dangers of secrecy, saying that "the possession of secrets acts like a psychic poison that alienates their possessor from the community."[106] Not only is the *content* of the secret poisonous but so is the affect it carries; thus, "to cherish secrets and hold back emotion is a psychic misdemeanour for which nature finally visits us with sickness."[107] Both forms of secrecy result in guilt and isolation.

Certainly this was the consequence for the four women who were silent witnesses to unacknowledged parental discord. This, then, isolated them from the outside, "normal" world, making them feel different and strange, and it also led to a repression of feelings that may well have been one of the decisive factors in their later alcoholism. For the interdiction of exposing the parental shadow seems to have led to a repression of individual shadow as well, repressions that finally erupted under the influence of Dionysos.

One could speculate that the secret drinking which is so much a part of alcoholism, particularly in women, may also be a continuation of feelings of guilt and sinfulness that a child inherits without understanding. On the other hand, as every phenomenon has both a negative and a positive side, there is also a beneficial aspect to this secrecy. If it isolates the individual and keeps her in a state of unconsciousness to protect the dreaded family shadow, it also may force her, by its very isolating effect, to go beyond a merely collective identity into a more individual one. When the women were at their alcoholic nadir of isolation and rejection—Solange reduced to drinking in sordid solitude and attempting suicide; Roberta divorced and falling down and calling long-distance in nightly blackouts; Noelle estranged from her husband but unable to leave the house and participate in any kind of outside life; Colette not knowing where her children were and threatened with divorce—when this point came, they were able to seek help, to join AA and then to *share* their secret alcoholic world.

As Jung says, "A secret shared with several persons is as beneficial as a merely private secret is destructive."[108] From sharing arose the original mystery cults and initiation rites that have always existed as a means to differentiate the individual from the "featureless flow of unconscious community life and thus from deadly peril to his soul."[109] One could conclude, therefore, that the original secret in these families, as toxic as it was in the life of the individual woman, eventually became a vital part of a transformative initiation process.

Summary

To sum up the family elements that I found in common among the four women interviewed, there is first of all a lack of positive mothering. Whether the mother was frankly hostile to her daughter, as in Solange or Noelle's case, or cold and mechanical, as in Colette's, or possessive and intrusive, as in Roberta's, none of the women experienced their mothers as providers of nurturing and maternal security or as positive feminine role models. That the deprivation was most severe for Noelle, and in no way compensated by the presence of a father, may explain why she had the most trouble accepting herself and establishing a real sense of individual identity. That Colette's mother, although conventional and rigid, was still the least harmful, overtly, to her daughter may explain why, despite her drinking and admitted frustrations, she is the one who has found the greatest satisfaction in being a mother as well as an attractive woman who enjoys the simple *fun* of being female.

Related to this common negative mother complex is a common positive father complex. But the father image is inflated and idealized far beyond the reality of the actual father. This would be a necessary compensation for the negative mother, a sort of overloading of the one positive parent. But it would also be a compensation in the daughter's psyche for the fact that the father was literally or figuratively absent from her childhood and did not provide much concrete support. Nature abhors a vacuum and the psyche will invent what it needs if reality does not provide it. Again, in the case of Noelle, after her father had died she was bound to idealize him even more, leading her in and out of two marriages and into a third that is still not very satisfactory. She illustrates very well Jung's words about the overheroic animus and the impossibility of a wom-

an's finding happiness with a real man as long as this internalized
image is so strong:

> It is all up with the man whom the whims of fortune bring into
> contact with this infantile woman: he will at once be made identical
> with her animus-hero and relentlessly set up as the ideal figure,
> threatened with the direst punishments should he ever make a face
> that shows the least departure from the ideal.[110]

To say that Noelle actually punished her men would be an exaggeration. The contrary would be nearer the truth—her wrath, at least
until she started drinking, was directed against herself. The result,
however, was the same: havoc in her relationships due to an inferior
sense of the feminine and an unattainable, overvalued masculine.

Roberta's reluctance to remarry may also come from this inner
animus hero who outdoes any real man. But through her work, she
is assimilating this complex and thus putting her animus to work for
her consciously. Both Solange and Colette, on the other hand, are
now happily married and say that this has happened since joining
AA. The ideal masculine has found an impersonal outlet in the
spiritual participation in AA and this has made relationship with a
real man possible. That each of their fathers, unlike Roberta's and
Noelle's, also contributed some positive warmth and interest while
they were growing up, probably accounts to a large extent for their
ability to deal more easily with the internal animus hero.

Finally, the four women studied were all children of difficult or
unhappy marriages, of parents very different in background or temperament and unable to make their difficulties conscious. Nor could
they, as individuals, admit certain aspects of themselves. Instead
they remained within their projections on each other and their persona images of themselves, choosing to ignore the conflict or to
escape—leaving the tensions of opposites unresolved so that the
child felt the division within herself. This constellated the sense of
family secret and shadow that was experienced by all the women
when they were little girls. It isolated them from the collective, and
forced upon them a refuge in unconsciousness that was to be continued in the use of alcohol as an anesthetic and a means to avoid pain
and problems.

Archetypal Motifs

Besides the common personal and psychological elements in the four
women's stories, there are also similar archetypal ones. First, of
course, the Apollonian-Dionysian tensions were prominent in their
"myths"—just as it was in the stories of the housewife and the singer
used to illustrate that particular point in chapter three.

Even before they began drinking, we can see that they were striving for certain Apollonian standards of perfection and "rightness," according to patriarchal Olympian values: Noelle, with her determination to be a "good" girl, working as a means to gain approval, marrying a man because he looked like a perfect "blond Greek god," and her still-present wish to be a "cool, flawless beauty"; Solange, determined to be a perfect wife to her second husband, according to the persona image she had of herself and of "the couple"; Colette, with her drive to achieve like a man, to be a perfect housekeeper, mother *and* professional woman; and Roberta, with her desire to be a perfect hostess for a perfect gentleman husband.

None of them basically questioned the values of the society they grew up in. They simply wanted to be the *best* in it, whether as partners to men or in their own right. They all wanted both to belong and to be outstanding, in keeping with certain high aspirations that were defined by Apollonian criteria. Their aspirations, however, were all the more rigid in that there was no strong masculine presence to humanize and moderate the ideals they strove for. They therefore had to choose the collective image of perfection and achievement, and this, unmitigated and unmoderated by a sense of individual reality, as women and as human beings, exposed them to its opposite, the Dionysian—the opposite that is always present and ready to take over when consciousness becomes too one-sided.

Not that Dionysos was totally absent from their lives before they drank. On the contrary, one sees him in Colette's desire to become an actress, in Solange's and Noelle's modeling careers, where, as Noelle says, "I could transform my walk and style with each outfit," reflecting the multiplicity and fantasy of the god. But these short-lived episodes were soon aborted by parental pressure to follow more conventional patterns, ones more suitable to a certain idea of feminine roles. Apollo won out and so Dionysos receded, only to return later, but this time in a more irresistible and disruptive form— as the god of alcoholism.

In their drinking stories, we see the classic Dionysian elements: Colette's fascination with the South African "dolce vita," the opposite of her sedate provincial society, her later daydreams of being and doing everything she wanted beyond the limits of her boring conventional life, and then her aggressive personality changes and lack of responsibility to her children and household; Roberta's sudden discovery that she could be charming as a hostess and then her increasing dependence, blackouts, loss of control at home by herself; Solange's liberation from her stifling home into a world of glamour and jet-setters, followed by Dionysian libations with her husband and then loneliness and near-death; Noelle's drift into ghostly-lover daydreams far from her disappointing, prosaic reality, her use of alcohol to inspire her to finish her housework, and then her personality changes from docile, sweet wife into sharp-tongued shrew.

To some extent all these women experienced the joyful, inspirational side of Dionysos as the Great Loosener, followed by the darker aspects of his madness, wildness and destructiveness. They were all devoted to Dionysos, members of his cult, and tied to him through secrecy, compulsiveness and adoration. As David Stewart says in *Thirst for Freedom,* "Addiction is like religion, with the same absoluteness and worship of something greater than oneself. The difference is that in religion there is free choice."[111]

In alcoholism, there is no free choice—as these women discovered. They were able to overcome it, however, and all found in AA the Apollonian spiritual values they had previously sought in vain. None have had slips and they are unanimous in saying that the Program changed their lives. They are even "grateful" to be alcoholics in order to belong to the AA group.

In Search of the Feminine

Finally, in my study of these four women, I looked for the elements that might come together to form a portrait of a certain kind of woman. I wanted to see if there was a *feminine archetypal pattern*— restricting myself to Greek mythology—behind the individual women who drink too much.

To do this, I needed more than the family history and even more than the drinking story. I had to find out what these women had been like as children and adolescents, what they had done in their lives and what they were like today. In short, I looked for common elements of temperament and experience.

What struck me, as far as their life stories were concerned, was the fact that all had been fairly lively little girls, expressing their individuality with a certain spunk and sense of adventure. None fit the model of the "good little girl" dressed in ribbons. On the contrary, Roberta, who ran away at age four, Colette, who achieved much more than what was expected from a mere girl, Solange, who ran away from the stifling atmosphere of a girls' school, and Noelle, who answered back in her "insolent" manner—all refused in some way the docile feminine roles of conventional little girls. But this spunkiness and nonconformism was either squelched, as in the case of Noelle, or simply given up in later adolescence; then they tried to fit in with the prevailing cultural model of pretty, popular teenagers, and succeeded.

This same pattern repeated itself when each one left home to work or to be married at an exceptionally young age. None remained dependent on their parents for longer than necessary. All, married or not, were active women who sought out work, even though financially it would not have been necessary.

In each case the first marriage was a failure. In fact, two of the four marriages were not even consummated. In a way, they were parentheses in the new life of freedom away from home. But most interestingly, the worst drinking began when the uncertainties of professional life became secondary and marriage brought material security. Along with this security, however, the women lost their own professional identities. Roberta stopped working and gave herself full-time to hostessing and gracious homemaking. Although she had begun to drink before, it was really only when she had no individual outside challenge that she became alcoholic. The same is true of Noelle. She had worked all her life and managed alone with a child in situations where many women would have foundered; she only succumbed to alcohol when she no longer had to work. Colette, too, drank alcoholically for the first time when faced with the exclusive role of mother and wife. Solange completely lost control when she married. With the exception of Noelle, they all drank before they were married and sometimes Dionysos was being lived through this drinking. But Dionysos only became really demonic once they were bound to the role of wife or mother or both.

Observing this and taking note of the tomboyishness and the desire for professional activity, it seems clear that the archetypal patterns personified by the Greek goddesses Hera and Demeter do not suit these women alcoholics. Although marriage, the domain of Hera, was tried at least twice by all four women, it never satisfied as an end in itself. In fact, the more the woman tried to make it one, throwing herself full-time into the role, the more she tended to be seduced away, like Minyos' daughters, by Dionysos.

Nor is motherhood, Demeter's strength, a fulfilling way of life for any of them. Colette admits how difficult she found it to have her life interrupted by babies, and although since AA she has gladly embraced the role and the *feelings,* it was not a natural instinct from the start. Noelle says much the same and both, like many alcoholic women, say that the hardest thing to forgive themselves for, in their drinking careers, was the neglect of their children, who suffered from their unwillingness or incapacity to be good mothers. Solange affirms frankly that she does not want children and is glad her husband already has his family. Roberta relates that having children is secondary to other aspects of her life.

As for Hestia, archetypal model of the homemaker, she exists in all of these women to some extent. They all enjoy their homes (now at least), and have made them pleasant places to be. But for none of them is "home and hearth" the dominant value. Hestia seems to be lived in a secondary fashion. Their reluctance to put more energy into the concrete home environment, however, may also come from the example of their mothers who had *only* that as an outlet for their creativity and for whom it was more an expression of an ambitious but frustrated animus than a deep relationship with "home."

Aphrodite, goddess of love, is not much in evidence either. Although fathers' daughters, these women are nevertheless not particularly "anima" women, happy to be "all things to all men."[112] While all are attractive, none, with the possible exception of Colette, seeks to dress in a provocative or seductive or coquettish way. On the contrary, in manner and dress they are rather on the classic, understated side. Furthermore, none—again with the exception of Colette—has been especially involved in various love affairs, even when drinking. Only Colette has this Aphrodite side; she lived it out particularly while drinking but it is still unmistakably there in her charm, genuine beauty and striking way of dressing.

What about Artemis, goddess of the woods? Artemis, who was born of Ares, god of war, and the Great Mother, is above all a virgin goddess, prototype of, and akin to, the Amazons.[113] Like the Amazons she needs no man, is capable of doing all masculine tasks. Furthermore, in mythology she is related to Dionysos. Like him, she is a divinity, not of Olympian calm and civilization, but of virgin and wild nature. Like him she is a huntress with a following of women huntresses. Dionysos' wet nurse Hipta is thought to be identical with the Anatolian chief goddess and thus revered by the matriarchal Amazons. Also like Dionysos, Artemis can be a *bacchante* and as such she storms about drunkenly with her bow and deadly arrows. For a woman, she is the anticollective, unconventional goddess, the one who does not define herself in terms of men and their values, does not submit to their desires or their laws.

Reflecting upon this I recalled the revolt of Solange from her girls' school, the running-away of four-year-old Roberta. But also the scholastic achievement of Colette, and the feeling of defiant ugliness that Noelle had as an adolescent, going through the phase of the ugly duckling, when she went out at night—Artemis' time.[114] I also recalled the ambitions they all had to be independent from their families, mistresses of themselves and to achieve masculine tasks in their jobs. Even the common first-failed-marriage seemed to hint at Artemis, as if there was something in these women that would not be joined and subservient to men. Certainly in their drinking behavior one sees Artemis the *bacchante*—the personality change, aggressiveness toward their husbands, neglect of their children—Artemis revolting against and disdaining the calm Olympian order of the patriarchal family.

And yet, the more I looked into this, the more I realized that

Artemis did not really fit. Certainly she is there, and she definitely has a dominant place in these women's psychology, more than any of the goddesses so far mentioned. But Artemis is above all a goddess of women, and all the women alcoholics I have observed and interviewed are first and foremost fathers' daughters. The relationship with matriarchal values, in such cases, is in the unconscious. Artemis would therefore be *an aspect of their shadows,* to come out in moments of strong emotion, with or without alcohol, while the conscious feminine ego would correspond more to the pattern personified by the goddess Athena.

Athena is a father's daughter par excellence. Sprung from the head of Zeus, "fully armed, with a mighty shout,"[115] she disowns any relationship to a maternal source and refuses marriage as well, reserving herself exclusively for her father. On Olympus, she stands second to Zeus, before even Apollo, his favorite son. If Apollo is the spokesman, Athena is Zeus' agent—founder of cities, goddess of wisdom and action combined; as Areia, goddess of war; as Ergane, goddess of handicrafts. All her functions concern the establishment and maintenance of Father Right. Finally, she is the protector of heroes, helping Perseus to slay the Gorgon by showing him how to use her shield to see the reflection and not to look the Gorgon in the eyes.[116]

All of these attributes can be seen in the lives and characters of the four women interviewed. In spite of some revolt against tradition, they essentially always sought to *belong* and felt unhappy at being outsiders. As children, then as workers and as wives, they wanted to be the *best,* according to collective standards. They even displayed "heroic" qualities in their professional and personal attempts to succeed. There is little trace of wild originality in their way of life or appearance, few hints of Amazon disdain for masculine systems.

On the other hand, they do not consider themselves inferior or subservient to men either. Like Athena, they see themselves as men's equals and seek out the company of men, much more than that of women. For all of them, men have been more important at turning points, never women. In their alcoholic drinking, they expressed a need to be like men, rather than choosing a more "feminine" illness, like hysteria. In AA they find acceptance as alcoholics and readily heed both the men and the Program. Some, "more royalist than the king," are in fact much more zealous in AA than many men are. But most of all, these women espouse the masculine way of doing things because it is natural for them, and they do not want to forego men in order to do so—as Artemis types might. On the contrary, as René Malamud points out in his article on Athena:

It belongs to her essence to associate herself with men, always thinking about them, always near them. She reveals herself to those who
are separated from the erotic not through prudery but through the
austerity and clarity of active effort.[117]

Thus, with their husbands they want to be partners, not just wives
and mistresses, mothers or housekeepers. The married ones have
"teamed up" with men in important positions, financially successful,
reflecting the values that Athena supports and encourages in her role
as representative of her father. The fact that they are married or
sexually active at all, and not virgin like Athena, simply reflects a
cultural situation in which solitary Athenas have less influence than
married ones and few women want to reject the traditional roles
altogether. Besides, literal virginity is not the point, as Esther Harding emphasizes in her psychological description of the virgin woman
as "one-in-herself," which the modern Athena aspires to be.[118]

The question that remains is: "Why, if these women are Athenas,
secure in their father's preference and in their role of creating and
maintaining his order, do they succumb to alcoholism, the opposite
of this?"

The answer may lie in the fact that their fathers were not very
satisfactory Zeus figures, and their mothers—negative figures like
Hera who resented the birth of Athena—nevertheless had the most
influence on their daughters, unlike the mythological Athena who
was protected by her father and had nothing to fear from the
enraged wife. The real women, born with Athenian temperaments
into less-than-Olympian circumstances, were obliged to put all their
energy into defending and maintaining the collective masculine,
more or less unmediated by the actual father. As Roberta so wist-
fully said, neither parent gave her any values and she regretted this.
Indeed, all were disappointed in and yet defended their fathers, but
they could only do so by espousing an idealized version.

As collective standards prove to be empty and sterile for the
individual who has only that, Athenian armor is bound to crack and
to be vulnerable to the Dionysian "Outsider," the one that Athena,
in fact, never allowed in her temple. But in the myth he came into
the house of Proitus and Minyos and took the women from their
"tasks of Athena and marriages of Hera," and one could suppose
that this happened because the tasks and the marriages had lost
their meaning and become mere roles adhered to for security, con-
venience or lack of consciousness.

Alcoholism is like an epidemic. In fact, today, it *is* epidemic. But
epidemics only strike those who have some kind of vulnerability,
which may be exposed through lowered resistance and negative
conditions. In this sense I think that the vulnerability—or predisposi-

tion—of many women alcoholics lies in a strong but unsupported Athenian temperament that is obliged to disguise itself in a Hera persona and an Apollonian animus because Athena, in the modern world, is not a valued model of the feminine. This, plus the growing-up in an emotionally difficult and unsupportive environment, drives such a woman to hang on to patriarchal values that are too general to be related to her own life; thus she is open to shadow attacks from her own Artemis side and the Dionysian energy that she has repressed or tried to hold at bay.

Were it not for Dionysos and the experience of living their shadows, however, the women whose stories I have presented would not have found an *authentic* Zeus-Olympus representation in AA, one that satisfies because it brings together both the necessary impersonal, transcendent values and the possibility of living these in relationship with other members, especially men—Athena's preferred companions.

Conclusion

This book has presented a look at alcoholism from various points of view, particularly as they apply to women. Beginning with an overview of generally accepted theories and attitudes, it has ended with a portrait of the alcoholic woman as one archetypally related to the aspirations and values of the Greek goddess Athena.

Athena, who is above all her father's daughter, who identifies with and defends his values; Athena who protects heroes and all the people and things concerned with the *polis,* the city, the civilized place. But human beings are not gods. They suffer when they become too one-sided, for more than one god should "live" through a human. As René Malamud points out in "The Amazon Problem" (quoting Artemis from Euripides' *Hipploytus*): " ... and there is a law among Gods, that no one of us should seek to frustrate another's purpose but let well enough alone."[119] So alcoholic women, in their unconscious one-sided Athena-ness, become subject to invasions from other sources, other gods—such as Artemis and Dionysos. But even within AA the basic temperament does not change, it is only transformed: the Athena values in the lives of recovered women alcoholics become truly theirs, and not just unconscious mimicry.

This does not necessarily lead to "the best of all possible worlds," however. Certainly it leads to a "better" one, in that the human woman, no longer obliged to drink, is able to live and function more fully as a sober individual and member of AA. Yet every god and goddess has its negative side, including Athena. Although the Athena tendencies of the woman drinker may help her to recover and to discover moderation, accept limits and extol consciousness, at the same time there is often a loss—a loss of wild, irrational, unexpected, anti-Olympian elements that drinking brought to the woman. This seems to happen through a reinforcement of her rational, Apollonian animus and the suppression of her destructive, but also potentially creative, Dionysian side. As Murray Stein remarks, referring to the dangers of too strong an Athena standpoint:

> For good and ill, the spirit of Athena enters therapy, or perhaps works to convert analysis into therapy, as analyst or analysand (or both) becomes compulsively interested in "improvement," "ego-building" action, heroic striving, patient effort for concrete results. . . . There is a demand to translate thought into action, to leave off wallowing in conflicts for decision, to convert insights into improved ego defenses.
> . . .
>   But because she has used the defense of identification with the aggressor [archaic Zeus, according to Stein], *she has no means left open for full expression of her womanhood. This is the trap of the soul which has chosen the defense of heroic striving.*[120]

Similar accusations could be leveled at AA methods. But for many women drinkers, this "trap" is nonetheless preferable to the pit of alcoholism. What is more, it is all the more preferable since it is a trap more suited to their Athena natures than any other— certainly an advance over the perfectionistic values of Apollo or the Dionysian lure of ecstatic irresponsibility. It may restrict them to being *only* themselves—as they adhere to the Olympian way that the AA Program reveals—but in this there is a unity, both inner and outer, that they never knew before.

Some women remain entirely satisfied within this unity, happy to "belong" at last and able to live without the crutch of alcoholism. If they feel some regrets, as Noelle expresses in her longing for "something exciting to happen," most would not go back to drinking to find it. As Colette says about her alcoholic fantasy world, "No thanks, the price is too high."

Others, though actively involved in the group work of AA, are more aware than ever of the "something missing" that alcohol once supplied (or covered up), and they look for this in more individual ways as well. Usually they find themselves attracted to some kind of creative activity that activates the unconscious—whether it be through analysis, a meaningful relationship, work or hobby. When this brings satisfaction, it is often because it has touched upon the other, non-Athena feminine values necessary to experience what Stein calls the "full expression of her womanhood." This is an individual issue, however, for if alcoholism may force the woman drinker into an attempt at recovery and transformation on one level, sobriety itself does not force every recovered alcoholic onto the road of individuation.

Alcoholics Anonymous, for a woman, is above all a way into a positive relationship with the collective, and especially the collective masculine. This is not bad, considering that most women, not only drinkers, suffer from feelings of being unaccepted in a masculine world.[121] But if that is AA's strength, it is also its limitation. For although AA may effect a reconciliation between Apollo and Dionysos and offer a healthier outlet for a woman's Athena nature, it is *not* a forum for all the gods, within or outside of Olympus. They must find other places, other means of expression.

Finally, it must be acknowledged that not all the millions of women alcoholics correspond to the model represented by Athena. But the examples I chose are of women who have *only* alcohol as an addiction or source of life-disrupting psychological problems. I know many other types of women who drink too much—more akin to Demeters, Hestias, Aphrodites, etc. But all, without exception, have either another addiction as well—drugs, food, pills—or some other form of severe psychic disturbance that is equal to or more important than the alcohol. I am convinced that the *alcoholic* aspect of a woman springs from her Athena side, and that this part can find help in AA. But the other gods or goddesses, so to speak, may be more important in her psyche than Athena, and these will manifest in other addictions or problems.

One sees many such women in AA, women who have a drinking problem like everyone else, but who somehow seem more complicated and/or problematical than others. Some manage to relate, through their Athena side, to the Program and indirectly this helps their other problems. Many do not, however. Either Athena is not strong enough in them to "convince" the other parts of their psyche that AA can help—in that case they just drop out, "inevitable casualties," spoken of as "those who can't make it"—or they do "make it," become sober, but continue to suffer, usually in silence, not quite like the others.

So far, AA is the only world-wide, long-term successful program for addicted people. Therefore, people with double addictions (if one is alcohol), will continue to seek help there. With luck, it will work at least for the alcohol. But not always, and not for everyone. In the very nature of the AA Program, it can *only* treat alcoholism and this very concentration, based on the precept "like cures like," is responsible for its success in that area. But double addiction, particularly pills-alcohol and food-alcohol, are becoming more and more frequent, especially among women. Where those with this problem can find support, equal to that of AA, remains to be discovered.

Appendix 1

Reproduced from AA Grapevine

The TWELVE STEPS

1. We admitted we were powerless over alcohol — that our lives had become unmanageable.

2. Came to believe that a Power greater than ourselves could restore us to sanity.

3. Made a decision to turn our will and our lives over to the care of God *as we understood Him*.

4. Made a searching and fearless moral inventory of ourselves.

5. Admitted to God, to ourselves, and to another human being the exact nature of our wrongs.

6. Were entirely ready to have God remove all these defects of character.

7. Humbly asked Him to remove our shortcomings.

8. Made a list of all persons we had harmed, and became willing to make amends to them all.

9. Made direct amends to such people wherever possible, except when to do so would injure them or others.

10. Continued to take personal inventory and when we were wrong promptly admitted it.

11. Sought through prayer and meditation to improve our conscious contact with God *as we understood Him*, praying only for knowledge of His will for us and the power to carry that out.

12. Having had a spiritual awakening as the result of these Steps, we tried to carry this message to alcoholics, and to practice these principles in all our affairs.

Reproduced from AA Grapevine

The
TWELVE
TRADITIONS

1. Our common welfare should come first; personal recovery depends upon AA unity.

2. For our group purpose there is but one ultimate authority — a loving God as He may express Himself in our group conscience. Our leaders are but trusted servants; they do not govern.

3. The only requirement for AA membership is a desire to stop drinking.

4. Each group should be autonomous except in matters affecting other groups or AA as a whole.

5. Each group has but one primary purpose — to carry its message to the alcoholic who still suffers.

6. An AA group ought never endorse, finance, or lend the AA name to any related facility or outside enterprise, lest problems of money, property, and prestige divert us from our primary purpose.

7. Every AA group ought to be fully self-supporting, declining outside contributions.

8. Alcoholics Anonymous should remain forever nonprofessional, but our service centers may employ special workers.

9. AA, as such, ought never be organized; but we may create service boards or committees directly responsible to those they serve.

10. Alcoholics Anonymous has no opinion on outside issues; hence the AA name ought never be drawn into public controversy.

11. Our public relations policy is based on attraction rather than promotion; we need always maintain personal anonymity at the level of press, radio, and films.

12. Anonymity is the spiritual foundation of all our Traditions, ever reminding us to place principles before personalities.

Appendix 3

The Bill W.—C.G. Jung Letters

From the January 1968 Grapevine

Here is a vital chapter of AA's early history, first published in the Grapevine in January 1963, and reprinted in January 1968. (Back copies of both issues have been entirely sold out.)

This extraordinary exchange of letters revealed for the first time, not only the direct historical ancestry of AA, but the bizarre situation wherein Jung, deeply involved with scientists and with a scientific reputation at stake, felt he had to be cautious about revealing his profound and lasting belief that the ultimate sources of recovery are spiritual sources. Permission to publish Dr. Jung's letter was granted to the Grapevine by the Jung estate.

January 23, 1961

My dear Dr. Jung:

This letter of great appreciation has been very long overdue.

May I first introduce myself as Bill W., a co-founder of the Society of Alcoholics Anonymous. Though you have surely heard of us, I doubt if you are aware that a certain conversation you once had with one of your patients, a Mr. Roland H., back in the early 1930's, did play a critical role in the founding of our Fellowship.

Though Roland H. has long since passed away, the recollection of his remarkable experience while under treatment by you has definitely become part of AA history. Our remembrance of Roland H.'s statements about his experience with you is as follows:

Having exhausted other means of recovery from his alcoholism, it was about 1931 that he became your patient. I believe he remained under your care for perhaps a year. His admiration for you was boundless, and he left you with a feeling of much confidence.

To his great consternation, he soon relapsed into intoxication. Certain that you were his "court of last resort," he again returned to your care. Then followed the conversation between you that was to become the first link in the chain of events that led to the founding of Alcoholics Anonymous.

My recollection of his account of that conversation is this: First of all, you frankly told him of his hopelessness, so far as any further medical or psychiatric treatment might be concerned. This candid and humble statement of yours was beyond doubt the first foundation stone upon which our Society has since been built.

123

Coming from you, one he so trusted and admired, the impact upon him was immense.

When he then asked you if there was any other hope, you told him that there might be, provided he could become the subject of a spiritual or religious experience—in short, a genuine conversion. You pointed out how such an experience, if brought about, might remotivate him when nothing else could. But you did caution, though, that while such experiences had sometimes brought recovery to alcoholics, they were, nevertheless, comparatively rare. You recommended that he place himself in a religious atmosphere and hope for the best. This I believe was the substance of your advice.

Shortly thereafter, Mr. H. joined the Oxford Group, an evangelical movement then at the height of its success in Europe, and one with which you are doubtless familiar. You will remember their large emphasis upon the principles of self-survey, confession, restitution, and the giving of oneself in service to others. They strongly stressed meditation and prayer. In these surroundings, Roland H. did find a conversion experience that released him for the time being from his compulsion to drink.

Returning to New York, he became very active with the "O.G." here, then led by an Episcopal clergyman, Dr. Samuel Shoemaker. Dr. Shoemaker had been one of the founders of that movement, and his was a powerful personality that carried immense sincerity and conviction.

At this time (1932-34), the Oxford Group had already sobered a number of alcoholics, and Roland, feeling that he could especially identify with these sufferers, addressed himself to the help of still others. One of these chanced to be an old schoolmate of mine, named Edwin T. ["Ebby"]. He had been threatened with commitment to an institution, but Mr. H. and another ex-alcoholic "O.G." member procured his parole, and helped to bring about his sobriety.

Meanwhile, I had run the course of alcoholism and was threatened with commitment myself. Fortunately, I had fallen under the care of a physician—a Dr. William D. Silkworth—who was wonderfully capable of understanding alcoholics. But just as you had given up on Roland, so had he given me up. It was his theory that alcoholism had two components—an obsession that compelled the sufferer to drink against his will and interest, and some sort of metabolism difficulty which he then called an allergy. The alcoholic's compulsion guaranteed that the alcoholic's drinking would go on, and the allergy made sure that the sufferer would finally deteriorate, go insane, or die. Though I had been one of the few he had thought it possible to help, he was finally obliged to tell me of my hopelessness; I, too, would have to be locked up. To me, this was a shattering blow. Just as Roland had been made ready for his conversion experience by you, so had my wonderful friend Dr. Silkworth prepared me.

Hearing of my plight, my friend Edwin T. came to see me at my home, where I was drinking. By then, it was November 1934. I had long marked my friend Edwin for a hopeless case. Yet here he was in a very evident state of "release," which could by no means be accounted for by his mere association for a very short time with the Oxford Group. Yet this obvious state of release, as distinguished from the usual depression, was tremendously convincing. Because he was a kindred sufferer, he could unquestionably communicate with me at great depth. I knew at once I must find an experience like his, or die.

Again I returned to Dr. Silkworth's care, where I could be once more sobered and so gain a clearer view of my friend's experience of release, and of Roland H.'s approach to him.

Clear once more of alcohol, I found myself terribly depressed. This seemed to be caused by my inability to gain the slightest faith. Edwin T. again visited me and repeated the simple Oxford Group formulas. Soon after he left me, I became even more depressed. In utter despair, I cried out, "If there be a God, will He show Himself." There immediately came to me an illumination of enormous impact and dimension, something which I have since tried to describe in the book *Alcoholics Anonymous* and also in *AA Comes of Age,* basic texts which I am sending to you.

My release from the alcohol obsession was immediate. At once, I knew I was a free man.

Shortly following my experience, my friend Edwin came to the hospital, bringing me a copy of William James's *Varieties of Religious Experience.* This book gave me the realization that most conversion experiences, whatever their variety, do have a common denominator of ego collapse at depth. The individual faces an impossible dilemma. In my case, the dilemma had been created by my compulsive drinking, and the deep feeling of hopelessness had been vastly deepened by my doctor. It was deepened still more by my alcoholic friend when he acquainted me with your verdict of hopelessness respecting Roland H.

In the wake of my spiritual experience, there came a vision of a society of alcoholics, each identifying with and transmitting his experience to the next—chain-style. If each sufferer were to carry the news of the scientific hopelessness of alcoholism to each new prospect, he might be able to lay every newcomer wide open to a transforming spiritual experience. This concept proved to be the foundation of such success as Alcoholics Anonymous has since achieved. This has made conversion experiences—nearly every variety reported by James—available on almost wholesale basis. Our sustained recoveries over the last quarter-century number about 300,000. In America and through the world, there are today 8,000 AA groups. [In 1974, worldwide membership is estimated to be 725,000; number of groups, nearly 22,500.]

So to you, to Dr. Shoemaker of the Oxford Group, to William James, and to my own physician, Dr. Silkworth, we of AA owe this tremendous benefaction. As you will now clearly see, this astonishing chain of events actually started long ago in your consulting room, and it was directly founded upon your own humility and deep perception.

Very many thoughtful AAs are students of your writings. Because of your conviction that man is something more than intellect, emotion, and two dollars' worth of chemicals, you have especially endeared yourself to us.

How our Society grew, developed its Traditions for unity, and structured its functioning, will be seen in the texts and pamphlet material that I am sending you.

You will also be interested to learn that, in addition to the "spiritual experience," many AAs report a great variety of psychic phenomena, the cumulative weight of which is very considerable. Other members have—following their recovery in AA—been much helped by your practitioners. A few have been intrigued by the *I Ching* and your remarkable introduction to that work.

Please be certain that your place in the affection, and in the history, of our Fellowship is like no other.

Gratefully yours,
William G. W—

*

January 30, 1961

Dear Mr. W.:
Your letter has been very welcome indeed.

I had no news from Roland H. any more and often wondered what has been his fate. Our conversation which he has adequately reported to you had an aspect of which he did not know. The reason that I could not tell him everything was that those days I had to be exceedingly careful of what I said. I had found out that I was misunderstood in every possible way. Thus I was very careful when I talked to Roland H. But what I really thought about was the result of many experiences with men of his kind.

His craving for alcohol was the equivalent, on a low level, of the spiritual thirst of our being for wholeness; expressed in medieval language: the union with God.

How could one formulate such an insight in a language that is not misunderstood in our days?

The only right and legitimate way to such an experience is that it happens to you in reality, and it can only happen to you when you walk on a path which leads you to higher understanding. You might be led to that goal by an act of grace or through a personal and honest contact with friends, or through a higher education of the mind beyond the confines of mere rationalism. I see from your letter that Roland H. has chosen the second way, which was, under the circumstances, obviously the best one.

I am strongly convinced that the evil principle prevailing in this world leads the unrecognized spiritual need into perdition if it is not counteracted either by real religious insight or by the protective wall of human community. An ordinary man, not protected by an action from above and isolated in society, cannot resist the power of evil, which is called very aptly the Devil. But the use of such words arouses so many mistakes that one can only keep aloof from them as much as possible.

These are the reasons why I could not give a full and sufficient explanation to Roland H., but I am risking it with you because I conclude from your very decent and honest letter that you have acquired a point of view above the misleading platitudes one usually hears about alcoholism.

You see, "alcohol" in Latin is *spiritus,* and you use the same word for the highest religious experience as well as for the most depraving poison. The helpful formula therefore is: *spiritus contra spiritum.*

Thanking you again for your kind letter,

I remain

yours sincerely
C.G. Jung

Notes

CW — *The Collected Works of C.G. Jung*

1. *New York Times Magazine,* July 1980.
2. E.g., Betty Ford, wife of U.S. President Gerald Ford, whose courageous admission of her alcohol problem went far to shatter some of the myths and stereotypes surrounding the woman alcoholic.
3. Neil Kessel and Henry Walton, *Alcoholism,* pp. 94-95.
4. David A. Stewart, *Thirst for Freedom,* p. 68.
5. Ibid., p. 55.
6. Quoted by Edward C. Whitmont in *Psyche and Substance,* pp. 119-120.
7. Henri F. Ellenberger, *The Discovery of the Unconscious,* pp. 240-243.
8. Ibid., p. 344.
9. Ibid., p. 345.
10. Ibid., p. 624.
11. Ibid., p. 285.
12. Jung, "Problems of Modern Psychotherapy," *The Practice of Psychotherapy,* CW 16, par. 172.
13. M. Siegler and H. Osmand, in *Quarterly Journal of Studies on Alcoholism,* vol. 29, no. 3.
14. *Alcoholics Anonymous,* pp. 171-177.
15. Kessel and Walton, p. 50.
16. Ruth Maxwell, *The Booze Battle,* p. 73.
17. Ibid., p. 77.
18. *AA Today,* pp. 31-33.
19. Ibid., pp. 33-35.
20. Ibid., p. 36.
21. "AA for the Woman," p. 3.
22. Siegler and Osmand, p. 10.
23. Ibid., p. 14.
24. Henry Ey, P. Bernard and Ch. Brisset, *Manuel de Psychiatrie,* p. 398. (Ed. trans.: "In the euphoria of drunkenness, he realizes, outside the constraints of the real world, the desires and dreams of an internal narcissistic and archaic world; he lives a dream of total power wherein he can happily annihilate the other, who has been experienced as a source of conflict.")
25. Ibid., p. 402. (Ed. trans.: "For the woman, drunkenness is rather a compensation for some failure or disappointment in her life — a deception, solitude, abandonment.")
26. Henderson and Gillespie, *Textbook of Psychiatry,* p. 416.
27. Ibid., p. 417.

28.   Kessel and Walton, pp. 55-62.

29.   Ibid., p. 59.

30.   Ibid., p. 61.

31.   Ibid., p. 115.

32.   Stewart, p. 55.

33.   See Appendix 3.

34.   Claude Steiner, *Games Alcoholics Play.*

35.   Jung, "The Theory of Psychoanalysis," *Freud and Psychoanalysis,* CW 4, pars. 307-311; see also his Introduction to Frances Wickes' *The Inner World of Childhood,* in *The Development of Personality,* CW 17, pars. 80-97.

36.   Jung, "On Manic Mood Disorder," *Psychiatric Studies,* CW 1, par. 190.

37.   Ibid., par. 220.

38.   Jung, "General Description of the Types," *Psychological Types,* CW 6, par. 573.

39.   Ibid., par. 805.

40.   Ibid., par. 804.

41.   Jung, *Psychology and Alchemy,* CW 12, par. 182.

42.   Ibid.

43.   Ibid.

44.   Jung, CW 17, par. 87; see also *Two Essays on Analytical Psychology,* CW 7, par. 240.

45.   Jung, "Basic Postulates of Analytical Psychology," *The Structure and Dynamics of the Psyche,* CW 8, par. 686.

46.   See Appendix 3.

47.   H. Strudwick, personal notes taken at Jung's "Interpretation of Visions" seminars. (An edited version of the complete seminars, 1930-1934, has been published by Spring Publications in two volumes under the title of *The Visions Seminars.*)

48.   Jung, CW 8, pars. 649-688.

49.   Ibid., par. 651.

50.   Ibid., par. 683.

51.   Jung, CW 17, par. 84.

52.   Ibid., par. 87.

53.   Jung, "The Family Constellation," *Experimental Researches,* CW 2, par. 1013.

54.   James Hillman, *Suicide and the Soul,* p. 38.

55.   Kessel and Walton, p. 91.

56.   Hillman, p. 17.

57.   Ibid., p. 50.

58.   Ibid., p. 53.

59. Ibid., p. 60.
60. Carl Kerényi, *The Gods of the Greeks*, pp. 133-142.
61. Ibid., p. 134.
62. Walter Otto, *Dionysus: Myth and Cult*, pp. 52-65.
63. Kerényi, *Gods of the Greeks*, p. 272.
64. Otto, p. 140.
65. Ibid., p. 141.
66. Ibid., p. 207.
67. Ibid., p. 205.
68. Ibid., p. 95.
69. Ibid., p. 171.
70. Jung, CW 6, par. 801.
71. Esther Harding, *The I and the Not I*, p. 72.
72. Ibid., p. 75.
73. Otto, pp. 172-173.
74. Ibid., p. 173.
75. Kerényi, *Gods of the Greeks*, p. 261.
76. Otto, p. 112.
77. Jung, CW 7, pars. 251-253.
78. Ibid., par. 252.
79. *Alcoholics Anonymous*, p. 282.
80. Jung, in *Spring 1939*, p. 122.
81. Jung, CW 3, par. 282.
82. See Carl Kerényi, *Asklepios: Archetypal Image of the Physician's Existence.*
83. Ibid., p. 17.
84. Ibid., p. 21.
85. Ibid., p. 22.
86. See Appendixes 1 and 2 for the complete Twelve Steps and Twelve Traditions.
87. Kerényi, *Asklepios*, p. 35.
88. See above, note 47.
89. Ibid.
90. Ibid.
91. Ibid.
92. Kerényi, *Asklepios*.
93. See Appendix 3.
94. Emma Jung, *Animus and Anima*, pp. 1-17.
95. Esther Harding, *The Way of All Women*, pp. 36-68.
96. Ibid., p. 72 (quoting Jung in *Civilization in Transition*, CW 10, par. 260).

97.   Ibid., p. 47.

98.   Emma Jung, p. 36.

99.   From "AA for the Woman."

100. Emma Jung, p. 33.

101. "AA for the Woman."

102. Ibid.

103. Emma Jung, p. 13.

104. See Carl Kerényi, "Kore," in Jung and Kerényi, *Essays on a Science of Mythology,* pp. 101-155.

105. Emma Jung, p. 17.

106. Jung, CW 16, par. 124.

107. Ibid., par. 132.

108. Ibid., par. 125.

109. Ibid., par. 124.

110. Jung, CW 5, par. 465.

111. Stewart, p. 32.

112. See Harding, *Way of All Women,* chapter 1: "All Things to All Men."

113. See René Malamud, "The Amazon Problem," in James Hillman, ed., *Facing the Gods,* pp. 47-65.

114. Like the young girls who in ancient Greece were put into the service of Artemis to live out their wild and uncouth sides before becoming women; see Carl Kerényi, "Mythological Images of Childhood," in Hillman, *Facing the Gods,* p. 42.

115. Robert Graves, *The Greek Myths,* vol. 1, p. 46.

116. See Carl Kerényi, *Athene: Virgin and Mother in Greek Religion.*

117. Malamud, p. 53 (quoting Walter Otto).

118. Esther Harding, *Woman's Mysteries: Ancient and Modern,* pp. 103, 105, 125.

119. Malamud, p. 64.

120. Murray Stein, "Translator's Afterthoughts," in Kerényi's *Athene,* pp. 76-77.

121. My impression is that men alcoholics more often experience a "total" spiritual transformation through AA than do women. This may be because they are already, simply by virtue of being male, accepted in a masculine world. Therefore, their alcoholism and recovery not only reintegrates them into the collective but also permits them to transcend collective standards by promoting the feeling and spiritual values that are so often denigrated in Western culture. In a man, these values are associated psychologically with the anima, his feminine soul.

Glossary of Jungian Terms

Anima (Latin, "soul"). The unconscious, feminine side of a man's personality. She is personified in dreams by images of women ranging from prostitute and seductress to spiritual guide (Wisdom). She is the eros principle, hence a man's anima development is reflected in how he relates to women. Identification with the anima can appear as moodiness, effeminacy, and oversensitivity. Jung calls the anima *the archetype of life itself.*

Animus (Latin, "spirit"). The unconscious, masculine side of a woman's personality. He personifies the logos principle. Identification with the animus can cause a woman to become rigid, opinionated, and argumentative. More positively, he is the inner man who acts as a bridge between the woman's ego and her own creative resources in the unconscious.

Archetypes. Irrepresentable in themselves, but their effects appear in consciousness as the archetypal images and ideas. These are universal patterns or motifs which come from the collective unconscious and are the basic content of religions, mythologies, legends, and fairytales. They emerge in individuals through dreams and visions.

Association. A spontaneous flow of interconnected thoughts and images around a specific idea, determined by unconscious connections.

Complex. An emotionally charged group of ideas or images. At the "center" of a complex is an archetype or archetypal image.

Constellate. Whenever there is a strong emotional reaction to a person or a situation, a complex has been constellated (activated).

Ego. The central complex in the field of consciousness. A strong ego can relate objectively to activated contents of the unconscious (i.e., other complexes), rather than identifying with them, which appears as a state of possession.

Feeling. One of the four psychic functions. It is a rational function which evaluates the worth of relationships and situations. Feeling must be distinguished from emotion, which is due to an activated complex.

Individuation. The conscious realization of one's unique psychological reality, including both strengths and limitations. It leads to the experience of the Self as the regulating center of the psyche.

Inflation. A state in which one has an unrealistically high or low (negative inflation) sense of identity. It indicates a regression of consciousness into unconsciousness, which typically happens when the ego takes too many unconscious contents upon itself and loses the faculty of discrimination.

Intuition. One of the four psychic functions. It is the irrational function which tells us the possibilities inherent in the present. In contrast to sensation (the function which perceives immediate reality through the physical senses) intuition perceives via the unconscious, e.g., flashes of insight of unknown origin.

133

Participation mystique. A term derived from the anthropologist Lévy-Bruhl, denoting a primitive, psychological connection with objects, or between persons, resulting in a strong unconscious bond.

Persona (Latin, "actor's mask"). One's social role, derived from the expectations of society and early training. A strong ego relates to the outside world through a flexible persona; identification with a specific persona (doctor, scholar, artist, etc.) inhibits psychological development.

Projection. The process whereby an unconscious quality or characteristic of one's own is perceived and reacted to in an outer object or person. Projection of the anima or animus onto a real women or man is experienced as falling in love. Frustrated expectations indicate the need to withdraw projections, in order to relate to the reality of other people.

Puer aeternus (Latin, "eternal youth"). Indicates a certain type of man who remains too long in adolescent psychology, generally associated with a strong unconscious attachment to the mother (actual or symbolic). Positive traits are spontaneity and openness to change. His female counterpart is the **puella,** an "eternal girl" with a corresponding attachment to the father-world.

Self. The archetype of wholeness and the regulating center of the personality. It is experienced as a transpersonal power which transcends the ego, e.g., God.

Senex (Latin, "old man"). Associated with attitudes that come with advancing age. Negatively, this can mean cynicism, rigidity and extreme conservatism; positive traits are responsibility, orderliness and self-discipline. A well-balanced personality functions appropriately within the puer-senex polarity.

Shadow. An unconscious part of the personality characterized by traits and attitudes, whether negative or positive, which the conscious ego tends to reject or ignore. It is personified in dreams by persons of the same sex as the dreamer. Consciously assimilating one's shadow usually results in an increase of energy.

Symbol. The best possible expression for something essentially unknown. Symbolic thinking is non-linear, right-brain oriented; it is complementary to logical, linear, left-brain thinking.

Transcendent function. The reconciling "third" which emerges from the unconscious (in the form of a symbol or a new attitude) after the conflicting opposites have been consciously differentiated, and the tension between them held.

Transference and countertransference. Particular cases of projection, commonly used to describe the unconscious, emotional bonds that arise between two persons in an analytic or therapeutic relationship.

Uroboros. The mythical snake or dragon that eats its own tail. It is a symbol both for individuation as a self-contained, circular process, and for narcissistic self-absorption.

Bibliography

AA Today (25th Anniversary Publication). Cornwall Press, Cornwall, N.Y., 1960.

"AA for the Woman." Alcoholics Anonymous World Services, Inc., New York, 1968.

Alcoholics Anonymous. Cornwall Press, Cornwall, N.Y., 1939.

Big Book. Alcoholics Anonymous Publishing, Inc., New York, 1955.

Ellenberger, Henri F. *The Discovery of the Unconscious,* Basic Books, New York, 1970.

Ey, Henry, P. Bernard and Ch. Brisset. *Manuel de Psychiatrie.* Masson et Cie., Paris, 1974.

Graves, Robert. *The Greek Myths,* vol. 1. Penguin Books, Harmondsworth, 1955.

Harding, Esther. *The I and the Not I* (Bollingen Series LXXIX). Princeton University Press, Princeton, 1973.

———. *Psychic Energy: Its Source and Its Transformation* (Bollingen Series X). Princeton University Press, Princeton, 1973.

———. *The Way of All Women.* Harper Colophon, Harper & Row, New York, 1975.

———. *Woman's Mysteries: Ancient and Modern.* Rider & Company, London, 1971.

Henderson and Gillespie. *Textbook of Psychiatry* (10th edition). Oxford University Press, London, 1975.

Hillman, James. *Suicide and the Soul.* Spring Publications, Zurich, 1976.

———, ed. *Facing the Gods.* Spring Publications, Dallas, 1980.

Jung, C.G. *The Collected Works* (Bollingen Series XX). 20 vols., trans. R.F.C. Hull, ed. H. Read, M. Fordham, G. Adler, Wm. McGuire. Princeton University Press, Princeton, 1953-1979.

———. *The Visions Seminars.* 2 vols. (From the Notes of Mary Foote.) Spring Publications, Zurich, 1976.

———, and C. Kerényi. *Essays on a Science of Mythology: The Myth of the Divine Child and the Mysteries of Eleusis.* Harper & Row, New York, 1949.

Jung, Emma. *Animus and Anima.* Spring Publications, Zurich, 1978.

Kerényi, C. *Asklepios: Archetypal Image of the Physician's Existence* (Bollingen Series LXV:3). Pantheon Books, New York, 1959.

———. *Athene: Virgin and Mother in Greek Religion.* Spring Publications, Zurich, 1978.

———. *Dionysos: Archetypal Image of Indestructible Life* (Bollingen Series LXV:2). Princeton University Press, Princeton, 1976.

———. *The Gods of the Greeks.* Thames and Hudson, 1974.

Kessel, N., and H. Walton. *Alcoholism.* Penguin Books, Middlesex, 1965.

Maxwell, Ruth. *The Booze Battle.* Praeger Publications, New York, 1976.

Otto, Walter. *Dionysus: Myth and Cult.* Indiana University Press, Bloomington, 1965.

Perera, Sylvia Brinton. *Descent to the Goddess: A Way of Initiation for Women.* Inner City Books, Toronto, 1981.

Siegler, M., and H. Osmand. "Models of Alcoholism," in *Quarterly Journal of Studies on Alcoholism.* Rutgers University Center of Alcohol Studies, New Brunswick, N.J., vol. 29, no. 3 (September 1968).

Steiner, Claude. *Games Alcoholics Play.* Ballantine Books, Random House, New York, 1977.

Stewart, David A. *Thirst for Freedom.* Hazelden, Center City, Mn., 1960.

Twelve Steps and Twelve Traditions. Alcoholics Anonymous Publishing, Inc., New York, 1953.

Whitmont, Edward C. *Psyche and Substance: Essays on Homeopathy in the Light of Jungian Psychology.* North Atlantic Books, Richmond, Ca., 1980.

Woodman, Marion. *The Owl Was a Baker's Daughter: Obesity, Anorexia Nervosa, and the Repressed Feminine.* Inner City Books, Toronto, 1980.

———. *Addiction to Perfection: The Still Unravished Bride.* Inner City Books, Toronto, 1982.

Index

addiction, 11-15, 17, 30, 32, 34, 38-39, 45, 49, 63, 103, 113, 120
Adler, Alfred, 16
Aesklepios, 51, 69-75, 78, 105
Alanon, 27, 40
alchemy, 14, 50
alcoholics: character traits, 11-14, 32, 35-37
  Gamma and Delta, 33-34
  and psychotherapy, 32, 34, 37-39, 49, 84-85, 102-107, 119-120
Alcoholics Anonymous: 9, 12, 16-18, 31, 34, 38-40, 42, 44, 46
  and Aesklepios, 51, 69-75, 78
  and Apollo, 64-65, 67-74, 111-120
  and Dionysos, 63-65, 78, 111-120
  as model, 24-28
  spiritual program, 26-28, 38, 46-47, 71-78, 107, 116-120
  success of, 25-28, 34, 120
  Twelve Steps, 46, 62-63, 67-68, 72-73, 121
  Twelve Traditions, 72, 122
  and women, 26-28, 60-75, 77-79, 89-90, 94-95, 100-101, 104, 107, 110-120, 132
  and wounded healers, 51, 71-72
alcoholism: Alcoholics Anonymous model, 24-28
  and animus, 75-78, 104-107, 110-111, 115, 118-119
  archetypal factors, 13-14, 45, 51-79, 102-120
  and Athena, 116-120

clinical aspects, 11-14
cultural factors, 9-11
dry moral model, 20-21
as family curse, 40-41
and family interaction, 17, 40-41
as *felix culpa,* 69, 104
and ghostly lover, 76-77, 85, 104, 112
and goddesses, 114-120
as illness, 17, 22, 24-31, 38-39, 46, 66, 74
as impairment, 17-19, 22, 29, 38, 42
Jung's views, 43-47, 126-127
lay models, 17-28, 45-46
medical models, 28-31, 38-39, 42
medical treatment, 28-31
and moralism/morality, 20-24, 29-31, 38-39, 42, 45-48
and neurosis, 32, 34-36, 40, 43-44, 48-49, 63
as pathology, 15-17
and personality types, 35-37
primary and secondary, 32, 34
professional models, 28-42, 47-49
psychiatric models, 32-42
psychoanalytic models, 32, 42
psychological factors, 32-42, 101-111
psychological models, 32-42
and psychotherapy, 32, 34, 37-39, 49, 84-85, 102-107, 119-120
reasons for, 12-13, 34-40
and secrecy, 8, 12, 20, 24, 34, 36, 58, 90, 93, 108-111, 113
and sexuality, 12, 23, 36, 115

137

Addiction to Perfection
The Still Unravished Bride

A Psychological Study by
Marion Woodman

12. Addiction to Perfection: The Still Unravished Bride.
Marion Woodman (Toronto). ISBN 0-919123-11-2. 208 pages. $12

"This book is about taking the head off an evil witch." With these words Marion Woodman begins her spiral journey, a powerful and authoritative look at the psychology and attitudes of modern woman.

The witch is a Medusa or a Lady Macbeth, an archetypal pattern functioning autonomously in women, petrifying their spirit and inhibiting their development as free and creatively receptive individuals. Much of this, according to the author, is due to a cultural one-sidedness that favors patriarchal values—productivity, goal orientation, intellectual excellence, spiritual perfection, etc.—at the expense of more earthy, interpersonal values that have traditionally been recognized as the heart of the feminine.

Marion Woodman's first book, *The Owl Was a Baker's Daughter: Obesity, Anorexia Nervosa and the Repressed Feminine,* focused on the psychology of eating disorders and weight disturbances.

Here, with a broader perspective on the same general themes, Marion Woodman continues her remarkable exploration of women's mysteries through case material, dreams, literature and mythology, in food rituals, rape symbolism, Christianity, imagery in the body, sexuality, creativity and relationships.

The final chapter, a discussion of the psychological meaning of ravishment (as opposed to rape), celebrates the integration of body and spirit and shows what this can mean to a woman in terms of her personal independence.

Studies in Jungian Psychology
by Jungian Analysts

LIMITED EDITION PAPERBACKS

Prices quoted are in U.S. dollars (except for Canadian orders)

1. **The Secret Raven: Conflict and Transformation.**
Daryl Sharp (Toronto). ISBN 0-919123-00-7. 128 pages. $10

A concise introduction to the application of Jungian psychology. Focuses on the creative personality—and the life and dreams of the writer Franz Kafka —but the psychology is relevant to anyone who has experienced a conflict between the spiritual life and sex, or between inner and outer reality. (Knowledge of Kafka is not necessary.) Illustrated. Bibliography.

2. **The Psychological Meaning of Redemption Motifs in Fairytales.**
Marie-Louise von Franz (Zurich). ISBN 0-919123-01-5. 128 pages. $10

A unique account of the significance of fairytales for an understanding of the process of individuation, especially in terms of integrating animal nature and human nature. Particularly helpful for its symbolic, nonlinear approach to the meaning of typical dream motifs (bathing, beating, clothes, animals, etc.), and its clear description of complexes and projection.

3. **On Divination and Synchronicity: Psychology of Meaningful Chance.**
Marie-Louise von Franz (Zurich). ISBN 0-919123-02-3. 128 pages. $10

A penetrating study of the meaning of the irrational. Examines time, number, and methods of divining fate such as the I Ching, astrology, Tarot, palmistry, random patterns, etc. Explains Jung's ideas on archetypes, projection, psychic energy and synchronicity, contrasting Western scientific attitudes with those of the Chinese and so-called primitives. Illustrated.

4. **The Owl Was a Baker's Daughter: Obesity, Anorexia Nervosa, and the Repressed Feminine.**
Marion Woodman (Toronto). ISBN 0-919123-03-1. 144 pages. $10

A pioneer work in feminine psychology, with particular attention to the body as mirror of the psyche in eating disorders and weight disturbances. Explores the personal and cultural loss—and potential rediscovery—of the feminine principle, through Jung's Association Experiment, case studies, dreams, Christianity and mythology. Illustrated. Glossary. Bibliography.

5. **Alchemy: An Introduction to the Symbolism and the Psychology.**
Marie-Louise von Franz (Zurich). ISBN 0-919123-04-X. 288 pages. $16

A lucid and practical guide to what the alchemists were really looking for— emotional balance and wholeness. Completely demystifies the subject. An important work, invaluable for an understanding of images and motifs in modern dreams and drawings, and indispensable for anyone interested in relationships and communication between the sexes. 84 Illustrations.

6. **Descent to the Goddess: A Way of Initiation for Women.**
Sylvia Brinton Perera (New York). ISBN 0-919123-05-8. 112 pages. $10

A timely and provocative study of women's freedom and the need for an inner, female authority in a masculine-oriented society. Based on the Sumerian goddess Inanna-Ishtar's journey to the underworld, her transformation through contact with her dark "sister" Ereshkigal, and her return. Rich in insights from dreams, mythology and analysis. Glossary. Bibliography.

7. The Psyche as Sacrament: C.G. Jung and Paul Tillich.
John P. Dourley (Ottawa). ISBN 0-919123-06-6. 128 pages. $10

An illuminating, comparative study showing with great clarity that in the depths of the soul the psychological task and the religious task are one. With a dual perspective, the author—Jungian analyst and Catholic priest—examines the deeper meaning, for Christian and non-Christian alike, of God, Christ, the Spirit, the Trinity, morality and the religious life. Glossary.

8. Border Crossings: Carlos Castaneda's Path of Knowledge.
Donald Lee Williams (Boulder). ISBN 0-919123-07-4. 160 pages. $12

The first thorough psychological examination of the popular don Juan novels. Using dreams, fairytales, and mythic and cultural parallels, the author brings Castaneda's spiritual journey down to earth, in terms of everyone's search for self-realization. Special attention to the psychology of women. (Familiarity with the novels is not necessary.) Glossary.

9. Narcissism and Character Transformation: The Psychology of Narcissistic Character Disorders.
Nathan Schwartz-Salant (New York). ISBN 0-919123-08-2. 192 pp. $13

An incisive and comprehensive analysis of narcissism: what it looks like, what it means and how to deal with it. Shows how an understanding of the archetypal patterns that underlie the individual, clinical symptoms of narcissism can point the way to a healthy restructuring of the personality. Draws upon a variety of psychoanalytic points of view (Jungian, Freudian, Kohutian, Kleinian, etc.). Illustrated. Glossary. Bibliography.

10. Rape and Ritual: A Psychological Study.
Bradley A. Te Paske (Minneapolis). ISBN 0-919123-09-0. 160 pp. $12

An absorbing combination of theory, clinical material, dreams and mythology, penetrating far beyond the actual deed to the impersonal, archetypal background of sexual assault. Special attention to male ambivalence toward women and the psychological significance of rape dreams and fantasies. Illustrated. Glossary. Bibliography.

11. Alcoholism and Women: The Background and the Psychology.
Jan Bauer (Zurich). ISBN 0-919123-10-4. 144 pages. $12

A major contribution to an understanding of alcoholism, particularly in women. Compares and contrasts medical and psychological models, illustrates the relative merits of Alcoholics Anonymous and individual therapy, and presents new ways of looking at the problem based on case material, dreams and archetypal patterns. Glossary. Bibliography.

12. Addiction to Perfection: The Still Unravished Bride.
Marion Woodman (Toronto). ISBN 0-919123-11-2. 208 pages. $12

A powerful and authoritative look at the psychology and attitudes of modern woman, expanding on the themes introduced in *The Owl Was a Baker's Daughter*. Explores the nature of the feminine through case material, dreams and mythology, in food rituals, rape symbolism, perfectionism, imagery in the body, sexuality and creativity. Illustrated.

13. Jungian Dream Interpretation: A Handbook of Theory and Practice.
James A. Hall, M.D. (Dallas). ISBN 0-919123-12-0. 128 pages. $12

A comprehensive and practical guide to an understanding of dreams in light of the basic concepts of Jungian psychology. Jung's model of the psyche is described and discussed, with many clinical examples. Particular attention to common dream motifs, and how dreams are related to the stage of life and individuation process of the dreamer. Glossary.

14. The Creation of Consciousness: Jung's Myth for Modern Man.
    Edward F. Edinger, M.D. (Los Angeles). ISBN 0-919123-13-9. 128
    pages. $12

An important new book by the author of *Ego and Archetype,* proposing a
new world-view based on a creative collaboration between the scientific
pursuit of knowledge and the religious search for meaning. Explores the
significance for mankind of Jung's life and work; discusses the purpose of
human life and what it means to be conscious; examines the theological and
psychological implications of Jung's master-work, *Answer to Job;* presents a
radical, psychological understanding of God's "continuing incarnation"; and
illustrates the pressing need for man to become more conscious of his dark,
destructive side as well as his creative potential. Illustrated.

15. The Analytic Encounter: Transference and Human Relationship.
    Mario Jacoby (Zurich). ISBN 0-919123-14-7. 128 pages. $12

A sensitive and revealing study that differentiates relationships based on
projection from those characterized by psychological distance and mutual
respect. Examines the psychodynamics activated in any intimate relationship, and particularly in therapy and analysis; summarizes the views of Jung
and Freud on identification, projection and transference-countertrans-
ference, as well as those of Martin Buber (I-It and I-Thou relationships);
and shows how unconscious complexes may appear in dreams and emotional reactions. Special attention to the so-called narcissistic transferences
(mirror, idealizing, etc.), the archetypal roots of projection and the significance of erotic love in the analytic situation. Glossary. Bibliography.

16. Change of Life: A Psychological Study of the Menopause.
    Ann Mankowitz (Santa Fe). ISBN 0-919123-15-5. 128 pages. $12

A detailed and profoundly moving account of a menopausal woman's
Jungian analysis, openly facing the fears and apprehensions behind the
collective "conspiracy of silence" that surrounds this crucial period of every
woman's life. Dramatically interweaves the experience of one woman with
more generally applicable social, biological, emotional and psychological
factors; frankly discusses the realities of aging, within which the menopause
is seen as a potentially creative rite of passage; and illustrates how the
menopause may manifest, both in outer life and in dreams, as a time of
rebirth, an opportunity for psychological integration and growth, increased
strength and wisdom. Glossary. Bibliography.

All books contain detailed Index

INNER CITY BOOKS
Box 1271, Station Q, Toronto, Canada M4T 2P4
(416) 927-0355